Word 2003: Basic

Student Manual

THOMSON

━━━━━━━━━★━━━━━━━━━ ™

COURSE TECHNOLOGY

Australia • Canada • Mexico • Singapore
Spain • United Kingdom • United States

Word 2003: Basic

VP and GM of Courseware:	Michael Springer
Series Product Managers:	Charles G. Blum and Adam A. Wilcox
Developmental Editor:	Laurie Perry
Keytester:	Bill Bateman
Series Designer:	Adam A. Wilcox
Cover Designer:	Abby Scholz

For more information contact:

Course Technology
25 Thomson Place
Boston, MA 02210

Or find us on the Web at: www.course.com

For permission to use material from this text or product, submit a request online at: www.thomsonrights.com

Any additional questions about permissions can be submitted by e-mail to: thomsonrights@thomson.com

Trademarks

Course ILT is a trademark of Course Technology.

Some of the product names and company names used in this book have been used for identification purposes only and may be trademarks or registered trademarks of their respective manufacturers and sellers.

Disclaimers

Course Technology reserves the right to revise this publication and make changes from time to time in its content without notice.

*The ProCert Labs numerical rating referenced is based on an independent review of this instructional material and is a separate analysis independent of Certiport or the Microsoft Office Specialist program.

Microsoft, the Office Logo, Excel, Outlook, and PowerPoint are either registered trademarks or trademarks of Microsoft Corporation in the United States and/or other countries. The Microsoft Office Specialist Logo is used under license from owner.

Certiport and the Certiport Approved Courseware logo are registered trademarks of Certiport Inc. in the United States and/or other countries.

Course Technology is independent from Microsoft Corporation or Certiport, and not affiliated with Microsoft or Certiport in any manner. While this publication may be used in assisting individuals to prepare for a Microsoft Office Specialist exam, Microsoft, Certiport, and Course Technology do not warrant that use of this publication will ensure passing a Microsoft Office Specialist exam.

ISBNs

   1-4188-8952-0 = Student Manual
   1-4188-8954-7 = Student Manual with CDs (student data and CBT)

Printed in the United States of America

 2 3 4 5 6 7 8 9 PM 08 07 06

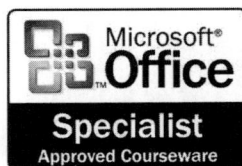

What does the Microsoft® Office Specialist Approved Courseware logo represent?

Only the finest courseware receives approval to bear the Microsoft® Office Specialist logo. In order to give candidates the greatest chance of success at becoming a Microsoft Office Specialist, all approved courseware has been reviewed by an independent third party for quality of content and adherence to exam objectives. This specific course has been mapped to the following Microsoft Office Specialist Exam Skill Standards:

- Word 2003 Specialist
- Word 2003 Expert

What is Microsoft Office Specialist certification?

Microsoft Office Specialist certification shows that employees, candidates and students have something exceptional to offer—proven expertise in Microsoft Office programs. Recognized by businesses and schools around the world, it is the only Microsoft-approved certification program of its kind. There are four levels of certification available: Specialist, Expert, Master, and Master Instructor.[1] Certification is available for the following Microsoft Office programs:

- Microsoft Word
- Microsoft PowerPoint®
- Microsoft Excel®
- Microsoft Outlook®
- Microsoft Access
- Microsoft Project

For more information

To learn more about becoming a Microsoft Office Specialist, visit www.microsoft.com/officespecialist.

To learn about other Microsoft Office Specialist approved courseware from Course Technology, visit www.course.com.

[1]The availability of Microsoft Office Specialist certification exams varies by Microsoft Office program, program version, and language. Visit www.microsoft.com/officespecialist for exam availability.

Contents

Introduction

After reading this introduction, you will know how to:

A Use Course Technology ILT manuals in general.

B Use prerequisites, a target student description, course objectives, and a skills inventory to properly set your expectations for the course.

C Re-key this course after class.

Topic A: About the manual

Course Technology ILT philosophy

Course Technology ILT manuals facilitate your learning by providing structured interaction with the software itself. While we provide text to explain difficult concepts, the hands-on activities are the focus of our courses. By paying close attention as your instructor leads you through these activities, you will learn the skills and concepts effectively.

We believe strongly in the instructor-led classroom. During class, focus on your instructor. Our manuals are designed and written to facilitate your interaction with your instructor, and not to call attention to manuals themselves.

We believe in the basic approach of setting expectations, delivering instruction, and providing summary and review afterwards. For this reason, lessons begin with objectives and end with summaries. We also provide overall course objectives and a course summary to provide both an introduction to and closure on the entire course.

Manual components

The manuals contain these major components:

- Table of contents
- Introduction
- Units
- Appendices
- Course summary
- Quick reference
- Glossary
- Index

Each element is described below.

Table of contents

The table of contents acts as a learning roadmap.

Introduction

The introduction contains information about our training philosophy and our manual components, features, and conventions. It contains target student, prerequisite, objective, and setup information for the specific course.

Units

Units are the largest structural component of the course content. A unit begins with a title page that lists objectives for each major subdivision, or topic, within the unit. Within each topic, conceptual and explanatory information alternates with hands-on activities. Units conclude with a summary comprising one paragraph for each topic, and an independent practice activity that gives you an opportunity to practice the skills you've learned.

The conceptual information takes the form of text paragraphs, exhibits, lists, and tables. The activities are structured in two columns, one telling you what to do, the other providing explanations, descriptions, and graphics.

Appendices

An appendix is similar to a unit in that it contains objectives and conceptual explanations. However, an appendix does not include hands-on activities, a summary, or an independent practice activity. We have also included an appendix that lists the Microsoft Office Specialist exam objectives for Microsoft Word 2003 along with references to corresponding coverage in Course ILT courseware.

Course summary

This section provides a text summary of the entire course. It is useful for providing closure at the end of the course. The course summary also indicates the next course in this series, if there is one, and lists additional resources you might find useful as you continue to learn about the software.

Quick reference

The quick reference is an at-a-glance job aid summarizing some of the more common features of the software.

Glossary

The glossary provides definitions for all of the key terms used in this course.

Index

The index at the end of this manual makes it easy for you to find information about a particular software component, feature, or concept.

Manual conventions

We've tried to keep the number of elements and the types of formatting to a minimum in the manuals. This aids in clarity and makes the manuals more classically elegant looking. But there are some conventions and icons you should know about.

Convention	Description
Italic text	In conceptual text, indicates a new term or feature.
Bold text	In unit summaries, indicates a key term or concept. In an independent practice activity, indicates an explicit item that you select, choose, or type.
`Code font`	Indicates code or syntax.
`Longer strings of ▶ code will look ▶ like this.`	In the hands-on activities, any code that's too long to fit on a single line is divided into segments by one or more continuation characters (▶). This code should be entered as a continuous string of text.
Select **bold item**	In the left column of hands-on activities, bold sans-serif text indicates an explicit item that you select, choose, or type.
Keycaps like (↵ ENTER)	Indicate a key on the keyboard you must press.

Hands-on activities

The hands-on activities are the most important parts of our manuals. They are divided into two primary columns. The "Here's how" column gives short instructions to you about what to do. The "Here's why" column provides explanations, graphics, and clarifications. Here's a sample:

Do it!

A-1:   Creating a commission formula

Here's how	Here's why
1 Open Sales	This is an oversimplified sales compensation worksheet. It shows sales totals, commissions, and incentives for five sales reps.
2 Observe the contents of cell F4	F4 ▼ = =E4*C_Rate The commission rate formulas use the name "C_Rate" instead of a value for the commission rate.

For these activities, we have provided a collection of data files designed to help you learn each skill in a real-world business context. As you work through the activities, you will modify and update these files. Of course, you might make a mistake and, therefore, want to re-key the activity starting from scratch. To make it easy to start over, you will rename each data file at the end of the first activity in which the file is modified. Our convention for renaming files is to add the word "My" to the beginning of the file name. In the above activity, for example, a file called "Sales" is being used for the first time. At the end of this activity, you would save the file as "My sales," thus leaving the "Sales" file unchanged. If you make a mistake, you can start over using the original "Sales" file.

In some activities, however, it may not be practical to rename the data file. If you want to retry one of these activities, ask your instructor for a fresh copy of the original data file.

Topic B: Setting your expectations

Properly setting your expectations is essential to your success. This topic will help you do that by providing:

- Prerequisites for this course
- A description of the target student at whom the course is aimed
- A list of the objectives for the course
- A skills assessment for the course

Course prerequisites

Before taking this course, you should be familiar with personal computers and the use of a keyboard and a mouse. Furthermore, this course assumes that you've completed the following courses or have equivalent experience:

- *Windows 2000: Basic*

Target student

You should have little or no experience with Word, but you should know how to use Windows and be somewhat familiar with file management concepts. By the end of this course, you should be able to use Word to create, open, format, save, and print a document.

Microsoft Office Specialist certification

This course is designed to help you pass the Microsoft Office Specialist exams for Word 2003. For complete certification training, you should complete this course as well as:

- *Word 2003: Intermediate*
- *Word 2003: Advanced*

Course objectives

These overall course objectives will give you an idea about what to expect from the course. It is also possible that they will help you see that this course is not the right one for you. If you think you either lack the prerequisite knowledge or already know most of the subject matter to be covered, you should let your instructor know that you think you are misplaced in the class.

Note: In addition to the general objectives listed below, specific Microsoft Office Specialist exam objectives are listed at the beginning of each topic. For a complete mapping of exam objectives to Course ILT content, see Appendix C.

After completing this course, you will know how to:

- Explain the Word environment; create, save, and close documents; and use the Help system.
- Navigate in a document; use some of Word's automated tasks; use basic editing techniques; and use the Undo and Redo commands.
- Select text; copy and move text; and use the Find and Replace commands to modify document text.

- Change the appearance of a document by applying character formats, by setting tabs, by aligning paragraphs and creating lists, and by setting paragraph indents and line spacing.
- Create, edit, and change the structure of tables in Word documents.
- Control page layout by adding headers and footers, setting page margins, and inserting page breaks.
- Proof a document by using the Spelling and Grammar checks; and preview and print a document.
- Save a Word document as an HTML file; view the HTML file in a browser; insert hyperlinks in documents; and send Word documents via e-mail.

Skills inventory

Use the following form to gauge your skill level entering the class. For each skill listed, rate your familiarity from 1 to 5, with five being the most familiar. *This is not a test.* Rather, it is intended to provide you with an idea of where you're starting from at the beginning of class. If you're wholly unfamiliar with all the skills, you might not be ready for the class. If you think you already understand all of the skills, you might need to move on to the next course in the series. In either case, you should let your instructor know as soon as possible.

Skill	1	2	3	4	5
Creating a document					
Saving and closing a document					
Entering text					
Previewing a document					
Using Help					
Navigating in a document					
Using AutoCorrect					
Deleting text					
Using Undo and Redo					
Selecting, moving, and copying text					
Finding and replacing text					
Formatting characters and paragraphs					
Setting tabs					
Creating and managing tables					
Adding headers and footers					
Working with margins and page breaks					
Checking spelling and grammar					
Using the Thesaurus					
Saving a document as an HTML file					
Inserting hyperlinks					
Sending Word documents via e-mail					

Topic C: Re-keying the course

If you have the proper hardware and software, you can re-key this course after class. This section explains what you'll need in order to do so, and how to do it.

Computer requirements

For you to re-key this course, your personal computer must have:

- A keyboard and a mouse
- Pentium 233 MHz processor (or higher)
- 128 MB RAM
- 1 GB of available hard drive space
- CD-ROM drive
- An SVGA monitor (800 x 600 minimum resolution support)
- A printer driver (An actual printer is not required, but you will not be able to complete the printing activities in Units 6 and 7 unless a driver is installed.)
- An active Internet connection

Setup instructions to re-key the course

Before you re-key the course, you will need to perform the following steps.

1 Install Microsoft Windows 2000 Professional on an NTFS partition according to the software manufacturer's instructions. Then, install the latest critical updates and service packs from www.windowsupdate.com. (You can also use Windows XP Professional, although the screen shots in this course were taken using Windows 2000, so your screens might look somewhat different.)

2 Adjust your computer's display properties as follows:

 a Open the Control Panel and double-click Display to open the Display Properties dialog box.

 b On the Settings tab, change the Colors setting to True Color (24 bit) and the Screen area to 800 by 600 pixels.

 c On the Appearance tab, set the Scheme to Windows Classic.

 d Click OK. If you are prompted to accept the new settings, click OK and click Yes. Then, if necessary, close the Display Properties dialog box.

3 Connect to the Internet. This course assumes that your computer is connected to the Internet, so some screens and activities might be different if it isn't connected.

4 Adjust the computer's Internet settings as follows:

 a On the desktop, right-click the Internet Explorer icon and choose Properties to open the Internet Properties dialog box.

 b On the Connections tab, click Setup to start the Internet Connection Wizard.

 c Click Cancel. A message box will appear.

 d Check "Do not show the Internet Connection wizard in the future" and click Yes.

 e Re-open the Internet Properties dialog box.

 f On the General tab, click Use Blank, click Apply, and click OK.

5   Install Microsoft Office 2003 according to the software manufacturer's instructions, as follows:

    a   When prompted for the CD Key, enter the 25-character code included with your software.

    b   Select the Custom installation option and click Next.

    c   Clear the check boxes for PowerPoint, Publisher, Access, and InfoPath.

    d   Select "Choose advanced customization of applications" and click Next.

    e   Next to Microsoft Word for Windows, click the drop-down arrow and choose Run all from My Computer.

    f   Next to Office Shared Features, click the drop-down arrow and choose Run all from My Computer.

    g   Next to Office Tools, click the drop-down arrow and choose Run all from My Computer.

    h   Click Next, and then click Install to start the installation.

6   If necessary, install a printer driver. If a printer was connected to the computer during the installation of Windows, there will be a driver installed for that printer. If not, you should install a standard PostScript printer driver, such as the HP LaserJet 5.

7   Start Word and do the following:

    a   Dock the Formatting toolbar below the Standard toolbar.

    b   Choose Tools, AutoCorrect Options to open the AutoCorrect: English (U.S.) dialog box. Then, verify/apply the following settings:

- On the AutoFormat As You Type tab, under Apply as you type, verify that Headings, Borders, Tables, Automatic bulleted lists, and Automatic numbered lists are checked.

- On the AutoFormat tab, under Apply, verify that Headings, Lists, Automatic bulleted lists, and Other paragraphs are checked.

- On the Smart Tags tab, under Recognizers, check Date (Smart tag lists).

    c   Click OK to close the dialog box.

8   Reset any Word default settings that you might have changed, or perform a fresh installation of Word according to the instructions in the preceding section. If you don't want to change your custom settings, some activities might not key properly. Settings that need to be reset include:

- Reset the Reading layout to display 2 pages (choose View, Reading Layout, and then click the Allow Multiple Pages button).

- Delete the AutoCorrect entries for "so" and "otulander."

- Delete the AutoText entry for "Good morning friends."

- Reset the Bullets and Numbering Gallery to the default settings.

- Remove "Financial" from the custom dictionary:

    a   Choose Tools, Options.

    b   On the Spelling & Grammar tab, click Custom Dictionaries.

    c   Click Modify and then delete the entry for "Financial."

9   Close Word.

10 Create a folder named Student Data at the root of the hard drive.

11 If necessary, download the Student Data files for the course. (If you do not have an Internet connection, you can ask your instructor for a copy of the data files on a disk.)

    a Connect to www.courseilt.com/instructor_tools.html.

    b Click the link for Microsoft Word 2003 to display a page of course listings, and then click the link for Word 2003: Basic, Second Edition.

    c Click the link for downloading the Student Data files, and follow the instructions that appear on your screen.

12 Copy the data files to the Student Data folder.

CertBlaster test preparation for Microsoft Office Specialist certification

If you are interested in attaining Microsoft Office Specialist certification, you can download CertBlaster test preparation software for Word 2003 from the Course ILT Web site. Here's what you do:

1 Go to www.courseilt.com/certblaster.

2 Click the link for Word 2003.

3 Save the .EXE file to a folder on your hard drive. (**Note**: If you skip this step, the CertBlaster software will not install correctly.)

4 Click Start and choose Run.

5 Click Browse and then navigate to the folder that contains the .EXE file.

6 Select the .EXE file and click Open.

7 Click OK and follow the on-screen instructions. When prompted for the password, enter **c_word**.

Unit 1

Getting started

Unit time: 45 minutes

Complete this unit, and you'll know how to:

A Use the elements of the Word window.

B Create and save documents.

C Access and use Help.

Topic A: Exploring the Word window

Explanation

Word 2003 is a word processing application that is part of the Microsoft Office suite. A *word processor* is a program that helps you create, edit, format, and print documents such as letters, reports, and Web pages. For example, you can create a project report in Word. While including project status information in the report, you might need to edit the report. You can edit the report by deleting text from it or by applying formatting to the text in the report. You can also insert graphics and charts, print the document, and save the finished report as an electronic file for future use.

Starting Word

To use Word, you must first start the application on your computer. To start Word, click the Start button and choose Programs, Microsoft Office, Microsoft Office Word 2003. When you start Word, a new blank document appears in the Word window.

Components of the Word window

Word has several components that help you interact with the program. Exhibit 1-1 shows some of these components.

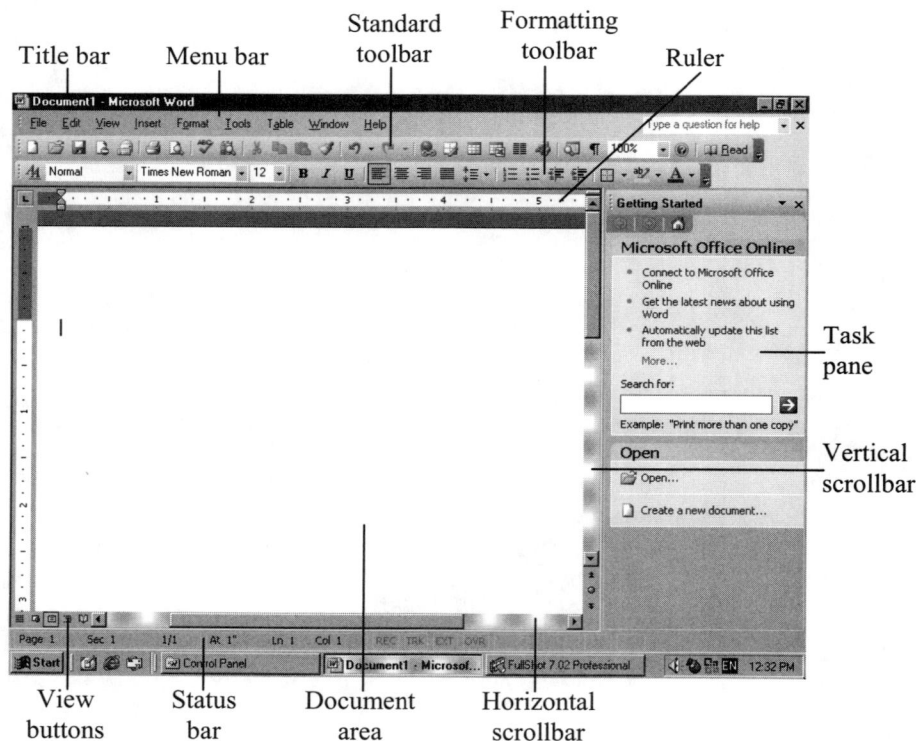

Exhibit 1-1: The components of the Word 2003 window

The following table explains the components of the Word window in detail:

Component	Description
Title bar	Displays the program title and the name of the current document.
Menu bar	Displays all menus available in Word. Each menu consists of a set of logically grouped commands.
Standard toolbar	Contains buttons for frequently used actions, such as opening files, saving files, and copying and pasting text. The buttons on this toolbar are shortcuts to the commands available in the menus.
Formatting toolbar	Contains buttons you can use for formatting text, such as changing font and font size. The buttons on this toolbar are shortcuts to the commands available in the menus.
Task pane	Provides shortcuts for performing commonly used commands, such as creating documents or formatting text. Located on the right side of the screen, the task pane changes depending on the current status of Word. Word provides 14 task panes. Some of the important task panes are Getting Started, Help, Search Results, Clip Art, Clipboard, Shared Workspace, Styles and Formatting, Mail Merge, XML Structure, and Protect Document.
Ruler	The horizontal and vertical rulers are used to set and view paragraph indents, tab stops, page margins, and column widths.
Document area	The document area is where you type and edit text. A flashing vertical line in the document area is called an *insertion point*. Below the insertion point is a small, black horizontal line called the *end-of-document marker*.
Scrollbars	You can use the horizontal and vertical scrollbars to move in a document, such as a multi-page report that cannot fit completely in the document area.
View buttons	View buttons are found to the left of the horizontal scrollbar. They help you change the view of the current document. The View buttons are Normal, Web Layout, Print Layout, Outline, and Reading Layout. These commands can also be found in the View menu.
Status bar	Displays information about the current document, such as the total number of pages, the number of the current page, and the position of the insertion point.

Do it!

A-1:   Starting Word and exploring the program window

Here's how	Here's why
1 Choose **Start**, **Programs**, **Microsoft Office**, **Microsoft Office Word 2003**	To start the Microsoft Word program. By default, a new document opens.
2 Observe the title bar	**Document1 - Microsoft Word**
	The title bar displays the current document's name (Document1) and the program name (Microsoft Word).
3 Observe the menu bar	(Located at the top of the Word window.) It contains commands that are used to perform actions in Word.
4 Choose **Insert**	To display the Insert menu. You can use the Insert menu commands to insert files, pictures, and other items into the current document. When you first display a menu, only the most common commands appear. You can either wait for the rest of the commands to appear, or click the double chevron at the bottom of the menu to display them.
Choose **Insert** again	To close the Insert menu.
5 Observe the toolbars	By default, the Standard and Formatting toolbars appear in the Word window.
Point to the first button on the Standard toolbar, as shown	New Blank Document
	After a moment, a ScreenTip appears, indicating that this is the New Blank Document button. You use this button to create a new document.
6 Observe the document area	This is where you create and edit documents.
7 Observe the insertion point	(The flashing vertical bar.) When you enter text in the document area, that text will appear to the left of the insertion point.
Move your mouse pointer to the insertion point	When you're in the document area, your mouse pointer looks like the letter I.

8	Observe the Getting Started task pane	(Located on the right side of the window.) The Getting Started task pane includes links for opening documents and creating new ones.
9	Observe the scrollbars	You use the horizontal scrollbar and the vertical scrollbar to scroll through a document. For example, if you have a multi-page report, it won't all be visible at once in the document area. So, to view various parts of the report, you can use the scrollbars.
10	Point to the first view button	 (At the far left of the horizontal scrollbar.) A ScreenTip indicates that this is the Normal View button.
11	Observe the status bar	(At the bottom of the Word window.) The status bar provides information about the current document and the current status of Word, such as the number of pages in the document and the page being viewed.

Topic B: Creating and saving documents

This topic covers the following Microsoft Office Specialist exam objectives.

#	Objective
WW03S-5-3	Creating and using folders for document storage
WW03S-5-3	Renaming folders
WW03S-5-7	Revealing formatting and hidden text (This objective is also covered in the unit titled "Formatting characters and paragraphs.")
WW03S-5-4	Converting documents to different formats for transportability (e.g., .rtf, .txt)

Creating a document

Explanation

You can create a new document in Word even when other documents are already open. To do so, click the New Blank Document button on the Standard toolbar, or choose File, New.

The New Blank Document button

Clicking the New Blank Document button creates a new document in the document area. The title bar displays a new document number.

The File, New command

The File, New command opens the New Document task pane, as shown in Exhibit 1-2. To create a new document, you click Blank document in the task pane. The task pane also contains links that can be used to open templates and wizards. These templates can be used to automate the creation of standard documents, such as reports, memos, faxes, and résumés.

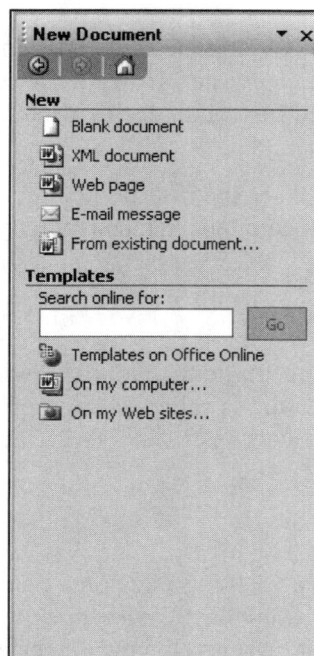

Exhibit 1-2: The New Document task pane

Do it!

B-1: Creating a new document

Here's how	Here's why
1 Choose **File**, **New...**	To open the New Document task pane, as shown in Exhibit 1-2. The New Document task pane appears at the right side of the Word window.
2 Click as shown	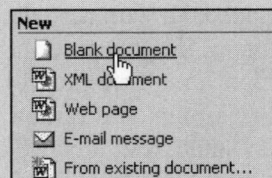
	(The Blank Document link is in the New Document task pane.) To create a document.
Observe the title bar	The name of the current document is "Document2." This is because when you open Word, a new document ("Document1") is open by default. The New Document task pane no longer appears in the Word window.

Adding text

Explanation

To enter text into a document, you type by using the keyboard. This process is similar to the way you'd create a document with a typewriter. However, Word has a large number of default settings that eliminate the need for you to decide what the text will look like and how it will be spaced on the page.

When you open a blank document, you'll see the insertion point. As you begin to type, the insertion point will move to the right, and the characters you type will appear to the left of the insertion point.

Word-wrap

As you reach the end of a line of text, you'll find that your text will automatically wrap to the next line of the document. This feature is called *word-wrap.* You can continue typing without pressing the Enter key to start a new line. By default, the word-wrap feature is activated in Word.

The Enter key

Pressing the Enter key is similar to using the Return key on a typewriter. Each time you press Return on a typewriter, you go to a new line. On a typewriter, you must use the Return key each time you reach the right margin. However, because word-wrap provides that function within Word, you need to use the Enter key in only three circumstances:

- To end a paragraph
- To end a line that does not reach the right margin
- To create a blank line in a document

Nonprinting characters

Word provides a feature called *nonprinting characters*, which are symbols that appear on the screen to represent actions on the keyboard. The Enter key, the Tab key, and the spacebar are all associated with nonprinting characters. These characters are called nonprinting because they appear only on the screen, not in the printed document. You might find them helpful when working with a document that contains a lot of formatting. You can turn these characters on or off by using the Show/Hide ¶ button on the Standard toolbar. Exhibit 1-3 shows a document with nonprinting characters.

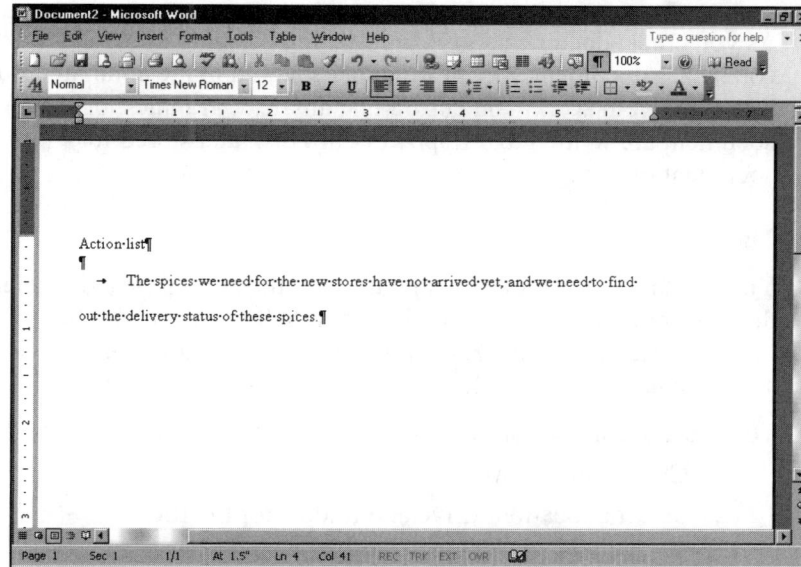

Exhibit 1-3: A document with nonprinting characters displayed

Do it!

B-2:   Entering text and displaying nonprinting characters

Here's how	Here's why
1 Observe the document area	The insertion point is flashing in the upper-left corner.
2 Type **Action list**	To see the text appear to the left of the insertion point.
3 Click ¶	(The Show/Hide ¶ button is on the Standard toolbar.) You'll see the nonprinting character for a paragraph mark at the end of the line you just typed.
4 Click ¶ again	To hide the nonprinting characters.
5 Display nonprinting characters	Click the Show/Hide ¶ button.
6 Press ⏎ ENTER twice	To insert two more paragraph marks.
7 Press TAB	This nonprinting character is called a tab mark. It indents the text on a page.
8 Type **The spices we need for the new stores have not arrived yet, and we need to find out the delivery status of these spices.**	The word-wrap feature will automatically move the text to the next line when you reach the right margin.

Saving a document

Explanation

As you create documents in Word, it's important to save your work frequently. Until you save a document, the information is stored in the computer's temporary memory. By saving your work, you ensure that any text, graphics, or other elements in your document are written to a floppy or hard disk and stored for future use. You save a document by using the Save and Save As commands.

The Save command

You use the File, Save command the first time you save a document. You can also use the Save button on the Standard toolbar. When you choose Save from the File menu in a new document, the Save As dialog box opens. You'll need to choose a location and specify a name for the file.

To save a document for the first time by using the Save command:

1 Choose File, Save.
2 Select a location (drive and folder) for the file.
3 Type a name for the file in the File Name box.
4 Click Save.

You can also use the Save command to save an existing document with its current name and in its current location. Essentially, the Save command updates a file, writing to the disk any changes that are still in computer memory. To save the changes in an existing document, you can either click the Save button on the Standard toolbar or press Ctrl+S.

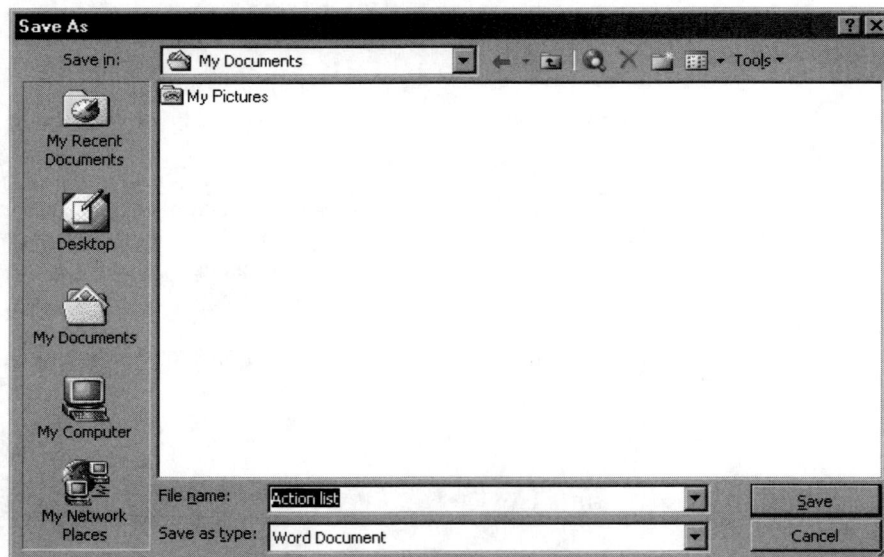

Exhibit 1-4: The Save As dialog box

Do it! **B-3: Saving a document by using the Save command**

Here's how	Here's why
1 Choose **File**, **Save**	To open the Save As dialog box, as shown in Exhibit 1-4. This dialog box appears when you save the document for the first time. By default, the Save As dialog box saves to the My Documents folder, and text in the File name box is highlighted.
2 Display the Save in list	(Near the top of the dialog box.) Click the down arrow next to the list.
Navigate to the current unit folder	You'll save the file in this folder.
3 Observe the File name box	(The File name box is in the Save As dialog box.) Word has named the file "Action list" based on the document text.
Observe the Save as type box	Your document will be saved as a Word document.
4 Click **Save**	To save your document with the name "Action list."
Observe the title bar	The title bar now displays "Action list" as the document name.

Creating a folder

Explanation

When you save your documents, you store them in folders on your local drive or on a network. The Save As dialog box can be used to save the document in a new folder. (Click the Create New Folder button in the Save As dialog box while you're saving the file.) You can also use the Save As dialog box to save a document with a new name.

To save a document in a new folder:

1   In the Save As dialog box, verify that the folder where you want to create a subfolder is selected in the Save in box.

2   Click the Create New Folder button to open the New Folder dialog box.

3   Enter the name of the new folder in the Name box.

4   Click OK to return to the Save As dialog box. The new folder is opened.

5   Enter the name for your file, and click Save to save the file to the new folder.

Converting a document to a different format

In the Save As dialog box, you can use the Save as type list to save a document in a different format, such as Rich-Text Format (.rtf) or Text Only (.txt). By doing so, the document will have a file name extension that is different from a Word document extension (.doc). Saving a document as a different type also enables you to send and share Word documents with other users who might not have access to Word.

Do it!

B-4:   Saving a document in a new folder

Here's how	Here's why
1 Choose **File, Save As...**	To open the Save As dialog box. The Save in list displays the current unit folder.
2 Click	(The Create New Folder button is at the top of the Save As dialog box.) The New Folder dialog box appears.
In the Name box, enter **My data**	To name the new folder as My data.
Click **OK**	The Save in box displays "My data."
3 Edit the File name box to read **My action list**	
Click **Save**	To save the document in the new folder. The new file name appears in the title bar.

Using Save AutoRecover

Explanation

When you're working, you might forget to save regularly. This means that you might lose your work from the last time you saved if the application closes unexpectedly. Word provides an automatic save feature that you can set to ensure that your documents are saved regularly. This feature is called Save AutoRecover and is found on the Save tab in the Options dialog box. You can specify, in minutes, how often Word should automatically save the file.

To specify the number of minutes between automatic saves:

1 Choose Tools, Options to open the Options dialog box.

2 Click the Save tab to view the various save options.

3 Check the Save AutoRecover info every box.

4 Use the spin controls to increase or decrease the minutes for the interval.

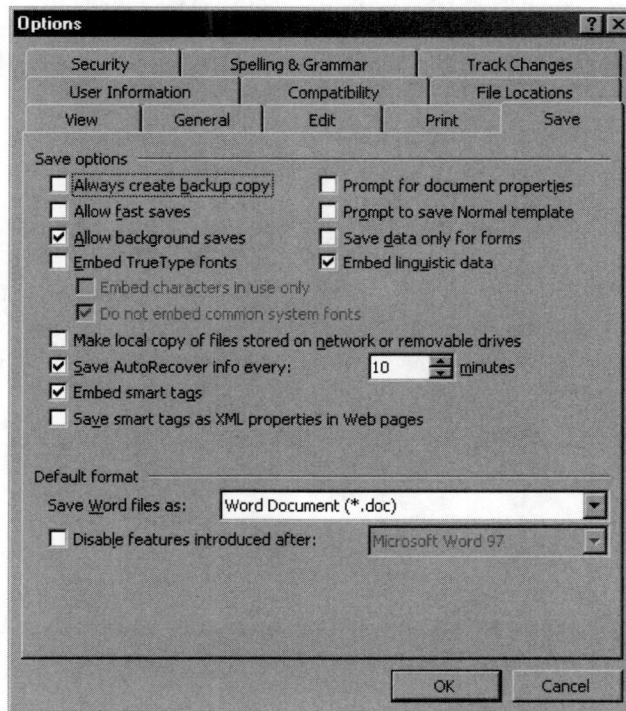

5 Click OK.

Exhibit 1-5: The Save tab in the Options dialog box

B-5:   Setting a Save AutoRecover time

Here's how	Here's why
1 Choose **Tools, Options...**	To open the Options dialog box.
2 Click the **Save** tab	To view the options in the Save tab, as shown in Exhibit 1-5.
Verify that Save AutoRecover info every is checked	This option is activated by default.
Set the time to **1** minute	Click the spin controls to decrease the number of minutes.
3 Click **OK**	To close the Options dialog box. Your documents will now be saved automatically after every minute.
4 Press ⏎ ENTER	To create a blank line in your document.
Press TAB	
5 Type **Get new tea list from Mary.**	To add a second action item to the list.
Observe the status bar	The save indicator appears on the status bar.
6 Click 💾	(The Save button is on the Standard toolbar.) To save the changes to your document, My action list.

Closing a document and Word

When you've finished working on a document, it's a good idea to close it until you need it again. If you haven't saved your document before you close it, Word prompts you to save before it closes the document.

You can close a document by clicking the Close button at the top of the document window or by choosing File, Close.

After you close a document, you can close Word. To do this, choose File, Exit.

Do it!

B-6:   Closing a document and closing Word

Here's how	Here's why
1 Choose **File**, **Close**	To close the document.
2 Choose **File**, **Exit**	(To close Word.) If prompted to save changes, click No.

Renaming folders

Explanation

To change the folder name, you must be in Windows Explorer. In addition, you must close all documents that relate to that folder. In Windows Explorer, navigate to the folder you intend to rename. You can either right-click the folder and choose Rename, or select the folder and choose File, Rename. When the folder name is highlighted, type the new name and press Enter.

Do it!

B-7:   Renaming a folder

Here's how	Here's why
1 Choose **Start**, **Programs**, **Accessories**, **Windows Explorer**	You can also right-click the Start button and choose Explore to start Windows Explorer.
Navigate to the Student Data folder	
Open the current unit folder	
2 Right-click **My data**	To display the shortcut menu for managing folders.
Choose **Rename**	The folder name is highlighted and ready for you to edit it.
Type your name	To personalize this folder.
Press (↵ ENTER)	To rename the folder.
3 Close Windows Explorer	Click the Close box in the upper-right corner of the window, or choose File, Close.

Topic C: Getting Help

This topic covers the following Microsoft Office Specialist exam objective.

#	Objective
WW03S-1-6	Locating supporting information in local reference materials or on the Internet using the Research tool

Help options

Explanation

You can use the Help system to access program information and instructions as you work. Word provides several tools to help you find what you need, including:

- The Type a question for help box
- The Office Assistant
- The Microsoft Word Help task pane

The Type a question for help box

To access help by using the Type a question for help box, type a question in the box and press Enter. It displays the related help topics in the Search Results task pane. Click any topic to display help in the Microsoft Word Help window.

Do it!

C-1: Using the Type a question for help box

Here's how	Here's why
1 Start Word	Click Start and choose Programs, Microsoft Office, Microsoft Office Word 2003.
Observe the right side of the menu bar	[Type a question for help ▼] To view the Type a question for help box.
2 Click the Type a question for help box	To place the insertion point in the box. The text "Type a question for help" disappears.
Enter **How do I copy a file?**	In the Type a question for help box.

3 Press ⏎ ENTER

Search Results   ▼ ✕

30 results from Office Online

- **Copy a file**
  Help > Moving, Copying, and Deleting Files

- **Open a backup copy of a document**
  Help > Document Backup

- **Print more than one copy**
  Help > Print Options

- **PDF Converter for Word: Convert PDF files directly into Word documents**
  Office Marketplace > Document Conversion and Imaging

- **Insert another file into an open document**

Search

Microsoft Office Online   ▼

How do I copy a file?   →

- Can't find it?

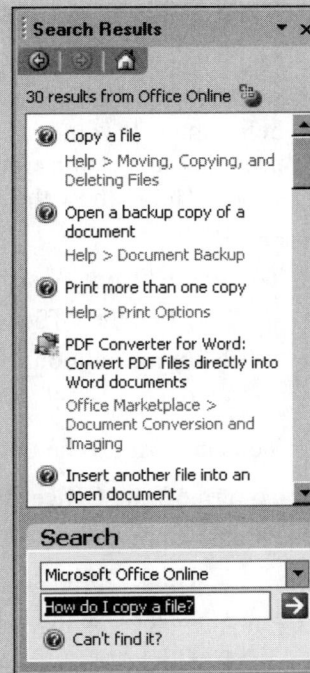

Search results appear in the Search Results task pane.

4 Click **Save a document**

To open the help topic in the Microsoft Word Help window. The Microsoft Word Help window appears on the right side of the Word window.

Close the Help window

Click the Close button in the upper-right corner of the Help window.

5 Observe the Type a question for help box

"How do I copy a file?" appears in the box. The topics on which you get help by using the Type a question for help box are appended to the list, which you can display by clicking the down arrow button to the right of the Type a question for help box. You can get help on these topics again by just selecting them from the list. The list gets refreshed every time you start Word.

The Office Assistant

Explanation

The Office Assistant is an animated help system that can answer questions while you work. Using the Office Assistant, you can type a question and then display the related help topics. If you don't find information related to the topic, the Office Assistant provides suggestions on how to phrase the question. To show the Office Assistant, choose Help, Show the Office Assistant. To hide it, choose Help, Hide the Office Assistant.

To use the Office Assistant:

1 Click the Office Assistant.

2 In the balloon, type a word or words relating to the topic you want help on.

3 Click Search.

You can turn off the Office Assistant if you don't need it.

To turn off the Office Assistant:

1 Right-click the Office Assistant.

2 Click Options.

3 Clear Use the Office Assistant.

4 Click OK.

Do it!   **C-2:   Using the Office Assistant**

Here's how	Here's why
1 Choose **Help, Show the Office Assistant**	To show the Office Assistant.
2 Click the Office Assistant	To display the "What would you like to do?" balloon.
3 In the box, type **Saving a file**	You'll find help on saving files.
Click **Search**	The Search Results task pane lists the Help topics that deal with saving files.
4 Click **Save a file**	The Microsoft Word Help window displays the information on the selected help topic. The Office Assistant is also visible.
5 Click the Office Assistant again	To display the Office Assistant balloon. In the question box, the text "Saving a file" appears.
Click **Options**	(On the "What would you like to do?" balloon.) To open the Office Assistant dialog box.
Clear **Use the Office Assistant**	To turn off the Office Assistant feature.
Click **OK**	To close the Office Assistant dialog box and turn off the Office Assistant.
6 Close the Help window	Click the Close button in the upper-right corner of the Help window.

The Microsoft Word Help task pane

Explanation

You can also get help on Word by using the Microsoft Word Help task pane. To open this task pane, choose Help, Microsoft Word Help. The Microsoft Word Help task pane has Assistance, Office Online, and See Also sections. You can use these sections to find relevant help topics.

If your computer is connected to the Internet, you can access related Microsoft sites by choosing Help, Office on Microsoft.com or by clicking the links in the Microsoft Word Help task pane. You can connect to the Microsoft Office Update site, get access to technical assistance and resources, view frequently asked questions, and e-mail questions to Microsoft support.

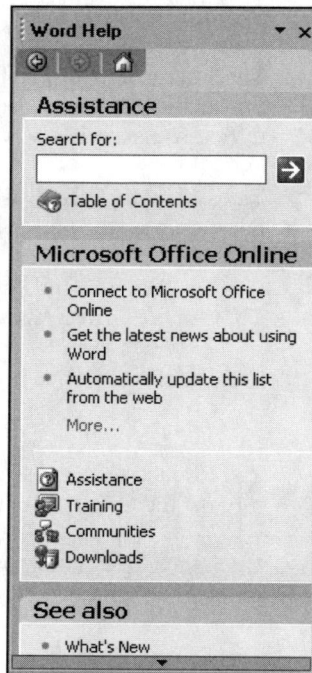

Exhibit 1-6: The Microsoft Word Help task pane

Do it!

C-3: Using the Microsoft Word Help task pane

Here's how	Here's why
1 Click [help icon]	(The Microsoft Word Help button is on the Standard toolbar.) To open the Microsoft Word Help task pane, as shown in Exhibit 1-6.
2 In the Search for box, enter **Saving a file**	To get help on saving a file.
Click [arrow icon]	(The Start searching button is to the right of the Search box.) The help topics related to the search text are displayed in the Search Results task pane.
3 Click **Save a document**	To display information on saving a document in the Microsoft Word Help window.
4 Close the Microsoft Word Help window	Click the Close button.
Close the Search Results task pane	Click the Close button in the upper-right corner of the task pane.
Close the document	Choose File, Close.

Unit summary: Getting started

Topic A

In this topic, you learned that Word 2003 is a word processor you can use to type, edit, format, and print documents. You started Word 2003 and explored the **Word 2003 environment**. You examined components of the Word window, including the title bar, menu bar, toolbars, ruler, status bar, document area, scrollbars, task pane, and View buttons. You entered text in a document by typing it in the document area. You also used the scrollbars to scroll through a document. You discovered that the Standard toolbar and the Formatting toolbar appear in the Word window by default.

Topic B

In this topic, you learned how to **create** and **save** documents. You saved a document by using the Save command in the File menu. You used the Save As command to save a document in a different folder and with a new file name. You also **renamed** a folder. You added text to a document and used the Enter key. You examined the nonprinting characters, which are symbols that represent keyboard actions, such as pressing the Enter key, the Tab key, or the spacebar.

Topic C

In this topic, you learned how to use the **Help** system by using the **Office Assistant**, the Type a question for help box, and the Microsoft Word Help task pane to find answers. You also discussed getting help on the Web.

Independent practice activity

1 Create a new document.

2 Type **I have learned the basics of using Word to create and save a document. I also know how to use Help**.

3 Save the document to the current unit folder as **My achievements**. (*Hint:* Use the Save command.)

4 Use the Type a question for help box to get help on opening a file.

5 Use the Microsoft Word Help task pane to find information about the same topic.

6 Select the topic called **Open a file**.

7 Close Help and the Search Results task pane.

8 Save your document in a new folder called **My new folder** under the current unit folder.

9 Close the document and Word.

Review questions

1 How is the File Save As command different from the File Save command?

2 What are nonprinting characters?

3 How are nonprinting characters displayed on screen?

4 Is it possible to create new folders from within Word? If so, how?

5 What feature enables you to automatically save documents and avoid data loss?

6 What is the procedure for renaming folders?

7 Name the ways to access help for Word.

8 How can you access on-line help for Word questions?

Unit 2

Editing documents

Unit time: 60 minutes

Complete this unit, and you'll know how to:

A Open and move around in a document.

B Use Word's automated tasks.

C Edit text in a document.

D Use the Undo and Redo commands.

Topic A: Opening and navigating in documents

This topic covers the following Microsoft Office Specialist exam objectives.

#	Objective
WW03S-1-3	Moving to selected content (e.g., Select Browse Object, Document Map) (This objective is also covered in *Word 2003: Intermediate*, in the unit titled "Working with styles.")
WW03S-5-7	Viewing reading layout, normal, outline, full screen, zoom views (This objective is also covered in the unit titled "Proofing and printing documents," as well as in the *Word 2003: Intermediate*, in the unit titled "Working with styles.")
WW03S-5-7	Showing/hiding white space in a document

Opening an existing Word document

Explanation

Opening a document means that you're retrieving it from the location on the disk where you saved it. When a document is opened, Word places a copy of it in the document window. The original document remains in the location where it was stored.

You open a file by using the File, Open command or by clicking the Open button on the Standard toolbar.

To open a file:

1. Choose File, Open or click the Open button to open the Open dialog box.
2. Navigate to the drive and folder where the file is located.
3. Select the file.
4. Click Open.

The Recently Used File list

The Recently Used File list provides a way to open any of the last four files you've worked on. This list is at the bottom of the File menu. To open a file from the list, choose File and select the file you want to open.

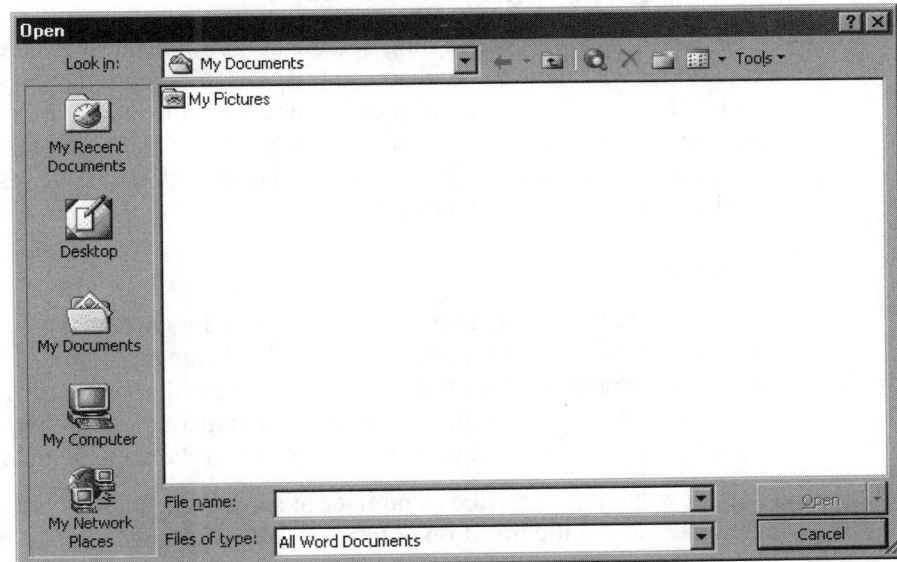

Exhibit 2-1: The Open dialog box

Do it!

A-1: Opening a file

Here's how	Here's why
1 Start Word	Click Start, and choose Programs, Microsoft Office, Microsoft Office Word 2003.
2 Choose **File**, **Open...**	The Open dialog box appears on your screen, as shown in Exhibit 2-1. You can navigate to different drives and folders by using the Open dialog box. You can also search for a file or files.
3 Navigate to the current unit folder	In the Look in list.
4 Select **Phase One**	
5 Click **Open**	The Phase One file appears on your screen in the document window. The name "Phase One" appears in the title bar.

Scrolling through a document

When you're working with a long document, you'll need to use the keyboard or the mouse to move around in the document. By default, Word displays about half of a standard 8.5" × 11" page. So if your document is longer than that, you'll need to use some navigation techniques to view all the content. There are several ways to scroll through a long document. You can use the horizontal and vertical scrollbars, the keys on your keyboard, or the Go To command.

Scrollbars

You use the horizontal and vertical scrollbars and your mouse to scroll through a document. *Scrollbars* are shaded bars displayed along the right side and the bottom of the document window. You use the horizontal scrollbar to scroll sideways. You use the vertical scrollbar to scroll the length of the document, page-by-page, screen-by-screen, or line-by-line. Exhibit 2-2 shows the elements of the vertical and horizontal scrollbars.

The following table describes a number of scrolling techniques. Note that none of these techniques moves the insertion point; they just change which part of the document is displayed.

Use this...	To do this...	By...
Up and down scroll arrows	Move up or down one line at a time	Clicking the arrows
Vertical scroll box	Move up or down in a document, to a specific page, or to a heading on a page	Dragging the box along the vertical scrollbar
Shaded areas above and below the vertical scroll box	Move up or down one screen at a time	Clicking the shaded area above or below the vertical scroll box
Left and right scroll arrows	Move left or right one character at a time	Clicking the arrow
Horizontal scroll box	Move left or right across a document	Dragging the box along the vertical scrollbar
Shaded areas to the left and right of the horizontal scroll box	Move left or right one screen at a time	Clicking the shaded area to the left or right of the horizontal scroll box

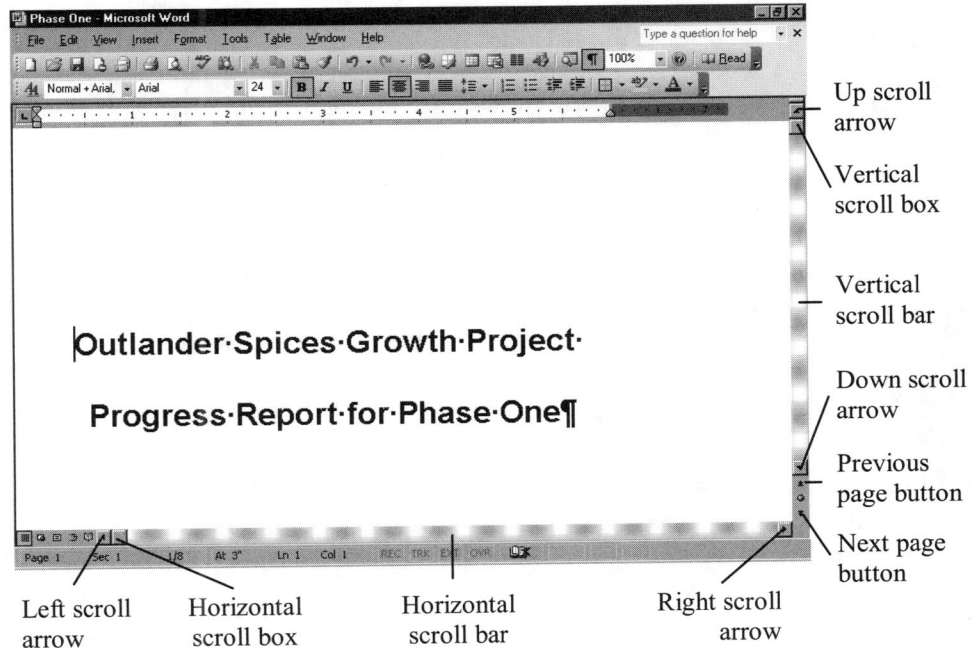

Exhibit 2-2: The elements of the horizontal and vertical scrollbars

Do it!

A-2:   Using scrollbars to navigate in a document

Here's how	Here's why
1 Click ▼	(The down scroll arrow is at the bottom of the vertical scrollbar.) To scroll down one line on the screen.
Click ▼ again	To scroll down another line.
2 Click the scrollbar below the vertical scroll box	To scroll down one screen in the document.
3 Point to the vertical scroll box, and press and hold the mouse	 A ScreenTip that displays the current page number appears.
Drag the scroll box to page 4	Point to the scroll box, press and hold the mouse button, and drag the box down the scrollbar.
4 Examine the horizontal scrollbar	You can use this scrollbar to move to the left and right of a document.
5 Return to the first page of the document	Drag the scroll box to the top of the vertical scrollbar.

Moving through documents

Explanation

You can use the keyboard or mouse to move through a document. When you *move* in the document, the insertion point moves corresponding to the text in the document area. The following table shows different movement techniques you can use to move in a document:

Use this...	To move...
←	To the previous character
→	To the next character
CTRL + ←	One word to the left
CTRL + →	One word to the right
↑	Up one line
↓	Down one line
CTRL + ↑	Up one paragraph
CTRL + ↓	Down one paragraph
HOME	To the beginning of a line
END	To the end of a line
CTRL + HOME	To the beginning of the document
CTRL + END	To the end of the document
PAGE DOWN	Down one page at a time
PAGE UP	Up one page at a time
⯅	To the top of the previous page (This button is below the vertical scrollbar.)
⯆	To the top of the next page (This button is below the vertical scrollbar.)

Do it!

A-3: Moving in a document

Here's how	Here's why
1 Press (PAGE DOWN)	To move down to the next page. The content in the document window has changed, and the insertion point has moved. The information displayed in the status bar changes to reflect the new location of the insertion point.
2 Click [▼]	(The Next Page button is below the vertical scrollbar.) To display the next page in the document window. The insertion point is flashing at the top of the page.
3 Press (PAGE UP)	To move up one page.
4 Press (CTRL) + (END)	To move to the end of the document. The insertion point is flashing at the end of the last word in the document window.
5 Click [▲]	(The Previous Page button is below the vertical scrollbar.) To move to the top of the previous page.
6 Press (CTRL) + (HOME)	To move to the beginning of the document. The insertion point is flashing to the left of the word "Outlander."

Using the Go To command

Explanation

In a long document, it can be time-consuming to move to a specific location by scrolling through the document or by using Page Up or Page Down. If you know the page number or line number you want to go to, you can use the Go To command to move quickly to that specific page, line, or other part of the document. The insertion point also moves when you use the Go To command, so you'll find it useful when you're editing a multi-page document.

The Go To command opens the Find and Replace dialog box, which displays the Go To tab. You can access the Go To tab of the Find and Replace dialog box in any of the following ways:

- Press F5.
- Choose Edit, Go To.
- Press Ctrl+G.

To use the Go To command to move to a specific page:

1   Press F5 (or choose Edit, Go To).
2   In the Enter page number box, type the number of the page you want to move to.
3   Click Go To.

Exhibit 2-3: The Go To tab in the Find and Replace dialog box

Do it!   **A-4:   Using the Go To command to move to a specific page**

Here's how	**Here's why**
1 Choose **Edit**, **Go To...**	To open the Find and Replace dialog box. The Go To tab is active.
2 Scroll through the Go to what list	Go to what: Page Section Line Bookmark Comment Footnote Endnote You'll see a list of options as to where you can move.
In the Go to what list, verify that Page is selected	
3 In the Enter page number box, enter **4**	As shown in Exhibit 2-3.
Click **Go To**	To move to page 4 of the document.
4 Click **Close**	To close the Find and Replace dialog box. The insertion point is flashing at the top of page 4.
5 Move to page 2	Use the Go To command.

The Select Browse Object button

Explanation

You can also move through a document by using the Select Browse Object button, which is located on the vertical scrollbar between the Previous and Next Page buttons. The term *object* refers to document elements such as pages, sections, comments, tables, or graphics.

Clicking the Select Browse Object button opens a menu that helps you choose an element of the document to browse. For example, if you choose Browse by Graphic, you'll go to the first graphic under the insertion point. You can then use the Previous and Next Page buttons to navigate from graphic to graphic. You can also access the Go To command by using the Select Browse Object button.

Do it!

A-5: Using the Select Browse Object button

Here's how	Here's why
1 Verify that the insertion point is at the beginning of page 2	Before the text, "Table of Contents."
2 Click ⊙	(The Select Browse Object button is between the Next Page and Previous Page buttons below the vertical scrollbar.) You'll see the Select Browse Object menu in the lower-right corner of your screen.
Point to different buttons on the menu	The name of each button appears at the bottom of the Select Browse Object menu box.
Select the option as shown	Browse by Graphic
	To browse by graphics. You've moved to the graphic on page 4.
3 Point to ⊼	The ScreenTip has changed to Next Graphic.
Click ⊼	To move to the next graphic on page 7.
4 Return the insertion point to the beginning of the document	Use any of the techniques you've learned to move the insertion point, along with the display in the document window.

Print Layout view

Explanation

Word provides different ways to view a document. Each view provides certain features that are useful for different types and lengths of documents. Normal view is the standard view that fills the screen from left to right and uses dotted lines to separate pages.

Print Layout view gives you a better sense of how the document will look when printed. As you scroll through a document, the whole page is shown, including all four edges. This can create a large amount of white space if a portion of the page is blank.

In Print Layout view, you can hide this extra white space. To do so, move the mouse pointer to the bottom or top edge of any page. When the mouse pointer becomes the Hide White Space tool, click it to hide the edges and extra white space. Solid black lines now separate the document pages. To unhide the white space, point to the solid black line, and when the mouse pointer displays Show White Space, click.

Do it!

A-6:   Using Print Layout view

Here's how	Here's why
1 Choose **View**	To display the View menu. Word provides different ways to view your document.
Choose **Print Layout**	To switch to Print Layout view. This view gives you a better sense of what your document will look like when it's printed.
2 Scroll through the document	For each page, you can see the four edges as well as white space near the top and bottom. This white space increases when pages contain small amounts of text. If the page is completely blank, it's still shown in Print Layout view.
3 Scroll to the bottom of any page	
Point to the bottom edge	
	The mouse pointer changes to the Hide White Space tool shown above.
Click the mouse	The white space is hidden, and a solid black line separates the pages.
4 Scroll through the document	The white space at the top and bottom of each page has been hidden.
5 Point to any solid black line	The mouse pointer changes to the Show White Space tool.
Click the mouse	To show the white space and return to Print Layout view.
6 Return the insertion point to the beginning of the document	If necessary.

Reading Layout view

Explanation

When you open a multi-page document, you can use the Reading Layout view. The Reading Layout view improves the readability of a document by hiding unwanted toolbars and automatically scaling text and graphics in a document. You can also highlight and review documents in Reading Layout view.

To switch to Reading Layout view, choose View, Reading Layout or click the Read button on the Standard toolbar. Exhibit 2-4 shows a document in the Reading Layout view. In this view, the document pages are referred to as *screens*. If only one screen appears in the view, you can click the Allow Multiple Pages button on the Reading Layout toolbar. You can scroll to view the other screens.

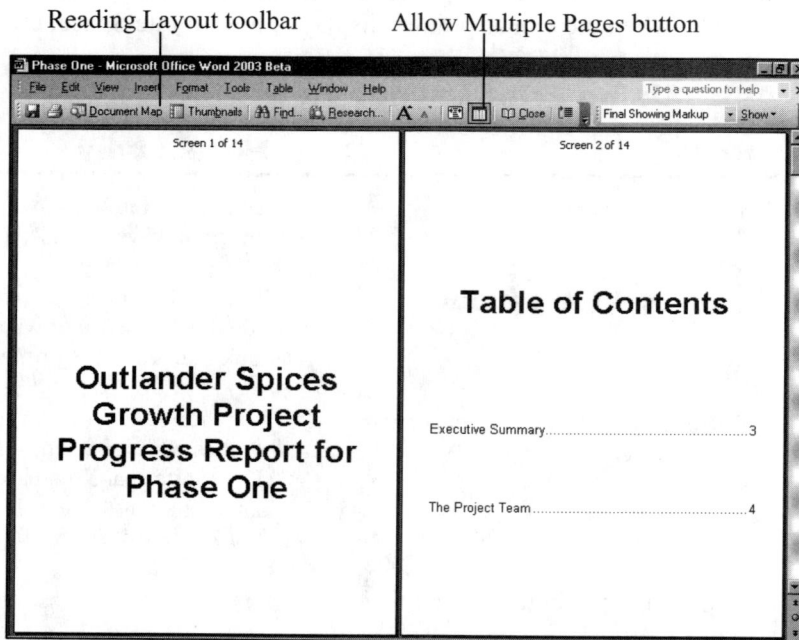

Exhibit 2-4: Reading Layout view

Do it!

A-7: Using Reading Layout view

Here's how	Here's why
1 Choose **View**, **Reading Layout**	To switch to Reading Layout view. The first two screens, or pages, appear.
2 Click ▼ twice	To view the next two screens in the document.
3 Click 📖	(The Allow Multiple Pages button is on the Reading Layout toolbar.) Only the third screen appears now.
Click 📖 again	To view the third and fourth screens of the document.
4 Click **Close**	(The Close button is on the Reading Layout toolbar.) To switch back to Normal view.
5 Close Phase One	(Choose File, Close.) If prompted to save changes, click No.

Topic B: Automated tasks

This topic covers the following Microsoft Office Specialist exam objectives.

#	Objective
WW03S-1-2	Creating text for repeated use (e.g., AutoText)
WW03S-1-2	Inserting pre-defined text (e.g., AutoText, AutoCorrect)

The AutoCorrect feature

Explanation

Automated tasks in Word include features such as AutoCorrect, AutoText, and AutoFormat. *AutoCorrect* corrects common errors as you type, such as misspelled words and incorrect capitalization.

AutoCorrect has several default entries that represent a list of common typing mistakes. It corrects these mistakes as soon as you press the Spacebar or type a punctuation mark. For example, if you type "bcak" instead of "back," AutoCorrect automatically replaces the misspelled word with the correctly spelled word when you press the spacebar or type any punctuation. In addition to correcting commonly misspelled words, AutoCorrect recognizes improper capitalization. For example, if you type "monday," AutoCorrect automatically capitalizes the first letter and changes the word to "Monday."

You can also use AutoCorrect to insert graphics or symbols in your document. AutoCorrect has a list of common symbols that you can insert by typing easier characters.

The following table shows some of these symbols:

Type this	AutoCorrect will insert this
(c)	©
(r)	®
(tm)	™

Do it!

B-1: Examining the AutoCorrect feature

Here's how	Here's why
1 Open a new document	Click the New Blank Document button on the Standard toolbar.
2 Choose **Tools**, **AutoCorrect Options...**	To open the AutoCorrect: English (U.S.) dialog box.
Verify that the AutoCorrect tab is active	
Examine the check boxes in the dialog box	By default, all the options are checked. You can choose which types of corrections AutoCorrect will make.
Verify that Replace text as you type is checked	This option tells AutoCorrect to correct your errors as you type.
3 Observe the Replace and With text boxes	You can add your own entries to AutoCorrect by using these boxes.
Scroll through the list of AutoCorrect entries	You'll see a list of commonly used symbols and common typing errors.
4 Click **Cancel**	To close the AutoCorrect: English (U.S.) dialog box.
5 Type **teh**	You're intentionally misspelling the word "the."
Press (SPACEBAR)	AutoCorrect automatically corrects the spelling of the word and capitalizes the "T" because this is the first word.
6 Press (↵ ENTER)	To create a blank line.
7 Type **Outlander Spices(TM)**	(TM) is the AutoCorrect entry for the trademark symbol. AutoCorrect automatically changes what you typed to the trademark symbol, ™.

The AutoCorrect Options button

Explanation

The AutoCorrect Options button appears near the text that has been automatically corrected. When you rest the mouse pointer over the corrected text, a button resembling a blue box appears. It changes to the button icon when you point to the automatically corrected text.

To undo the corrections made to the text, click the AutoCorrect Options button and select Undo Automatic Corrections.

You can turn off automatic capitalization of the first letter of sentences. You can also turn off the default AutoCorrect options by clicking the AutoCorrect Options button and selecting Control AutoCorrect Options.

Do it!

B-2:   Using the AutoCorrect Options button

Here's how	Here's why
1 Point as shown	The·¶ Outlander·Spices™¶ A blue box appears when you point to the automatically corrected word.
2 Point to the blue box	The blue box changes to the AutoCorrect Options button.
Click ⚡ ▾	⚡ ▾ nder·Spices™¶ ↶ Undo Automatic Corrections Stop Auto-capitalizing First Letter of Sentences Stop Automatically Correcting "teh" ⚡ Control AutoCorrect Options... To display the AutoCorrect Options list. The list shows the options to undo the automatic correction, stop capitalizing the first letter of sentences, and stop correcting the word "teh."
Choose **Undo Automatic Corrections**	The word is replaced by "teh" again.
3 Click the AutoCorrect Options button	
Choose **Redo Automatic Corrections**	To correct the word again.

Adding an AutoCorrect entry

Explanation

You can create your own AutoCorrect entries for typing errors you might make. You can also create an AutoCorrect entry that replaces an abbreviation with a word or words you type frequently. For example, you can create an AutoCorrect entry to automatically replace your initials with your name.

To add an entry to AutoCorrect:

1 Choose Tools, AutoCorrect Options to open the AutoCorrect: English (U.S.) dialog box.

2 In the Replace box, enter the word or words for the entry you want to create.

3 Press Tab to move the focus to the With box.

4 In the With box, enter the abbreviation you want to use.

5 Click OK.

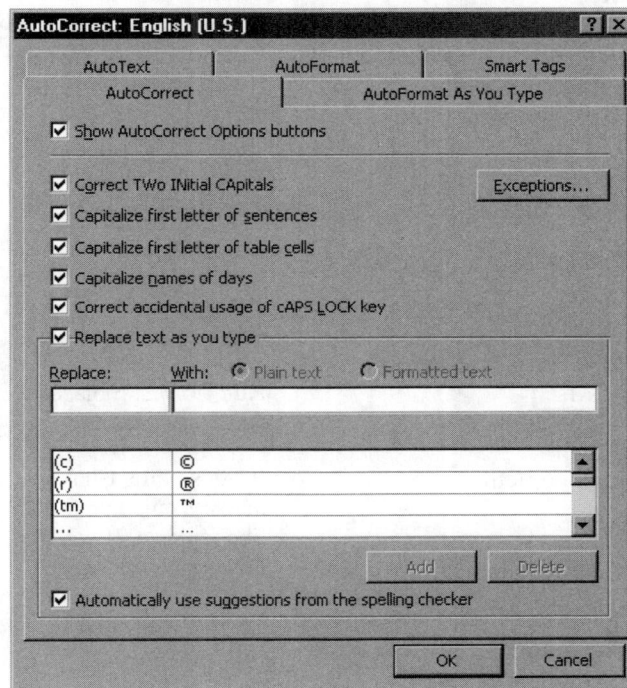

Exhibit 2-5: The AutoCorrect: English (U.S.) dialog box

Do it!

B-3:   Adding an entry to your AutoCorrect list

Here's how	Here's why
1 Choose **Tools**, **AutoCorrect Options...**	To open the AutoCorrect: English (U.S.) dialog box, as shown in Exhibit 2-5.
2 In the Replace box, enter **os**	The initials of the company Outlander Spices.
Press (TAB)	To move to the With box.
Type **Outlander Spices**	You'll create an AutoCorrect entry that will replace the letters "os" with the company name.
Click **Add**	To add the entry to the AutoCorrect list.
3 Click **OK**	To save the entry and close the AutoCorrect: English (U.S.) dialog box.
4 Place the insertion point at the end of the last paragraph	If necessary.
Press (↵ ENTER)	To insert a blank line.
5 Type **os**	Only the occurrences of "os" as the entire word will be automatically corrected. Word will not change "os" if it appears in the middle of a word.
Press (↵ ENTER)	AutoCorrect replaces the letters with the company name.
6 Close the document	(Choose File, Close.) Word recognizes that you haven't saved your document and asks if you'd like to do so. If you click Yes, the Save As dialog box opens.
7 Click **No**	To close the document without saving your changes.

Using AutoText

Explanation

You can use *AutoText* to insert predefined text entries, such as salutations, headers, footers, and signatures. Word provides AutoText entries for several commonly used phrases. You can also create your own AutoText entries.

The AutoText feature tries to anticipate what you want to say. The AutoText entries are grouped into categories such as Salutation, Closing, and Mailing Instructions.

For example, many business letters begin with "Dear Madam or Sir." As you type the first letters, Word recognizes this as a salutation and displays a suggested way to finish the phrase. This suggestion is called an *AutoComplete suggestion*. You can either accept the suggestion or ignore it and continue typing.

There are several ways to insert an AutoText entry:

- Choose Insert, AutoText, and select the preferred entry from the category submenu, as shown in Exhibit 2-6.
- Display the AutoText toolbar, click the All Entries button, and select the preferred entry from the category submenu.
- Begin typing. When the proper AutoComplete suggestion appears, press Enter or F3.

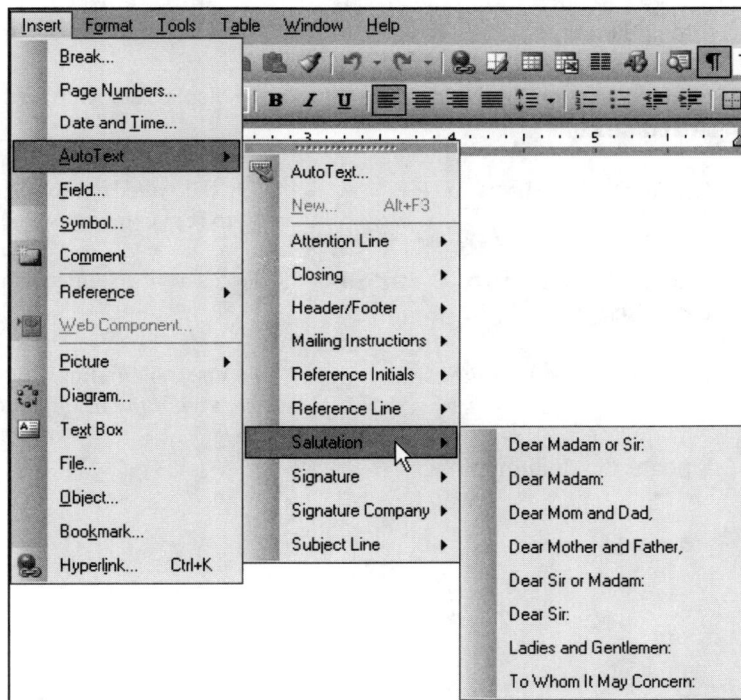

Exhibit 2-6: The cascading Insert, AutoText, Salutation menu

B-4: Using AutoText to enter standard text in a letter

Here's how	Here's why
1 Create a new document	You'll insert AutoText in this document.
Save the document as **My letter**	In the current unit folder.
2 Choose **Insert, AutoText**	To display the submenu of AutoText categories.
Choose **Salutation**	Dear Madam or Sir: Dear Madam: Dear Mom and Dad, Dear Mother and Father, Dear Sir or Madam: Dear Sir: Ladies and Gentlemen: To Whom It May Concern: To display the submenu with predefined salutations.
Close the menu	Click anywhere in the blank document.
3 Choose **View, Toolbars, AutoText**	To display the AutoText toolbar.
Click **All Entries**	(On the AutoText toolbar.) To display a menu of AutoText categories.
4 Choose **Salutation, Dear Sir or Madam:**	To insert this salutation in your document.
5 Press ⏎ ENTER twice	To insert blank lines to separate the salutation from the body of the letter.
Update the document	

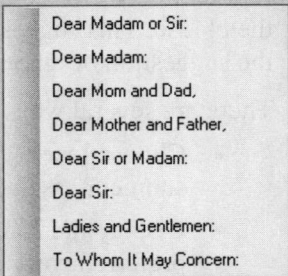

Creating new AutoText entries

Explanation   You might want to create an AutoText entry for a frequently used phrase. You can do so by using the AutoText tab of the AutoCorrect dialog box, as shown in Exhibit 2-7. To do so:

1   Choose Insert, AutoText, AutoText to open the AutoCorrect dialog box with the AutoText tab activated. (You can also click the AutoText button on the AutoText toolbar.)

2   In the Enter AutoText entries here box, type the text you want to insert as AutoText.

3   Click Add to add the new entry to the list.

4   Click OK.

By default, new entries are placed in the Normal category.

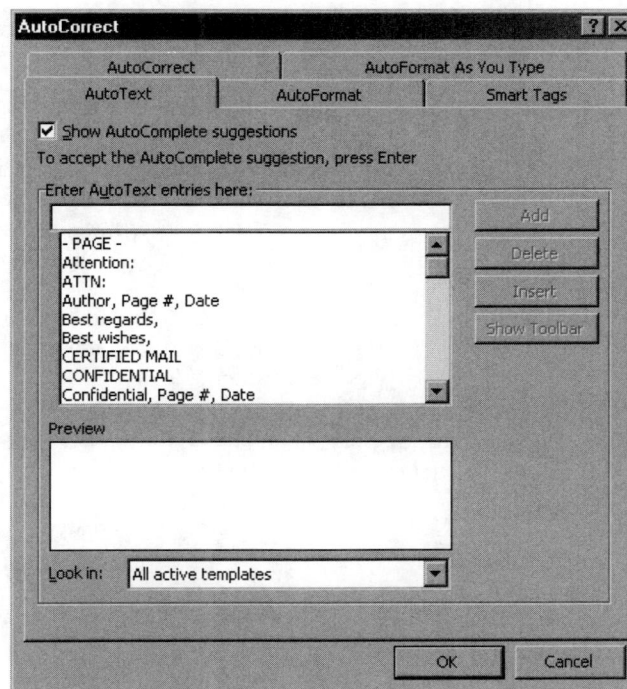

Exhibit 2-7: The AutoCorrect dialog box with the AutoText tab active

Do it!   **B-5: Creating an AutoText entry**

Here's how	Here's why
1 Click ⌨	(The AutoText button is on the AutoText toolbar.) To display the AutoCorrect dialog box with the AutoText tab activated.
2 In the Enter AutoText entries here box, enter **Good morning friends,**	┌─Enter AutoText entries here:─────┐ │ Good morning friends, │ └──────────────────────────────┘ This is the new AutoText entry.
Click **Add**	To add the AutoText entry to the list.
Click **OK**	To close the AutoCorrect dialog box.
3 Type **Good**	┌─Good morning friends, (Press ENTER to Insert)┐ │ Good¶ │ └──────────────────────────────┘ The ScreenTip "Good morning friends, (Press ENTER to Insert)" appears. You can press Enter or F3 to accept the suggested entry. If you don't want to insert the suggested entry, you can ignore it and continue typing.
Press (↵ ENTER)	To insert the AutoText in the document. You'll see that "Good morning friends," is typed automatically.
4 On the AutoText toolbar, display the Normal category entries	(Click All Entries to display the menu, and then choose Normal.) Your new entry has been added to the Normal category, which was created when the entry was created.
Close the menu	
5 Update and close the document	

Using AutoFormat

Explanation

You use the *AutoFormat* feature to apply formatting—such as headings, bulleted and numbered lists, borders, symbols, and fractions—based on the AutoFormat settings in the AutoCorrect dialog box. In the AutoFormat dialog box, you can specify the document type so that Word can apply the formats suitable for that type. For example, you can specify whether the document is a letter, an e-mail message, or a general document. You can use AutoFormat to format the entire document, or you can review each change suggested and choose whether to accept or reject it.

To AutoFormat a document:

1   Choose Format, AutoFormat to open the AutoFormat dialog box.

2   Select AutoFormat now to automatically format the entire document. You can also choose to review each proposed change.

3   Select General document, Letter, or E-mail as the document type.

4   If necessary, use the Options button to change the AutoFormat settings in the AutoCorrect dialog box.

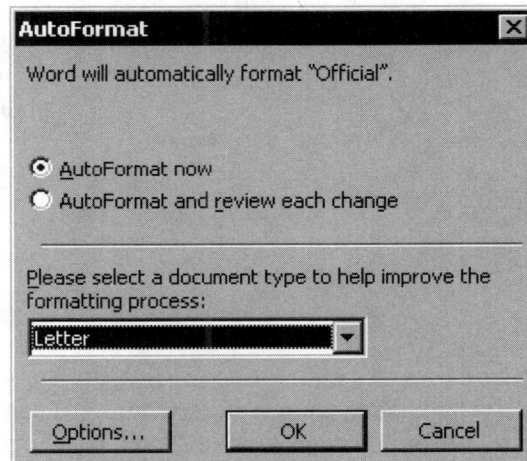

5   Click OK.

Exhibit 2-8: The AutoFormat dialog box

B-6: Using AutoFormat to format a document

Here's how	Here's why
1 Open Official	From the current unit folder.
Save the document as **My official**	
Scroll through the document	With the exception of bullets, this letter contains less formatting. You'll use the AutoFormat command to apply formatting.
2 Choose **Format**, **AutoFormat...**	To open the AutoFormat dialog box. You can choose to apply all AutoFormats now or review each suggested format before applying it. By default, AutoFormat now is selected.
3 From the list, select **Letter**	To format the document as a letter. Your screen should match Exhibit 2-8.
Click **OK**	To automatically format the document as a letter. A heading style is applied to Outlander Spices, Overview, and Closing, and the address fields in the upper part of the page are enclosed in a shaded box.
Update the document	

Click and Type

The *Click and Type* feature provides a way to insert text, graphics, and other items in a document with automatically applied paragraph formatting. When you move the mouse in a document, the mouse pointer changes to indicate the type of paragraph formatting that will be applied when you double-click. For example, when you point to the center of the page, the mouse pointer changes to an I-beam with a center alignment icon. If you double-click there, the text will be centered automatically.

By default, the Click and Type feature is enabled in Word. However, to take advantage of it, you must be in either Print Layout view or Web Layout view. The Click and Type feature does have some limitations. You cannot use it in multiple columns, bulleted and numbered lists, next to floating objects, or to the left or right of indents.

You can deactivate the Click and Type feature on the Edit tab of the Options dialog box. In addition, you can select the default paragraph style to be used. By default, the Normal style is selected.

Do it!

B-7:   Using Click and Type

Here's how	Here's why
1 Switch to Print Layout view	(If necessary.) Click the Print Layout View button to the left of the horizontal scrollbar.
2 Place the insertion point at the end of the document	
3 Move the mouse pointer around the blank area in the lower part of the page	The shape of the pointer changes as you move around the screen.
4 Double-click in the center of the page	(Approximately one inch below the last paragraph.) The insertion point is automatically centered on the page in the location you clicked.
Type **Thank** and press ⬤ SPACEBAR	The AutoText suggestion "Thank you," appears.
Press ⬤ ⏎ ENTER	To insert the AutoText entry.
5 Double-click as shown	

From·the·bottom·of·our·hearts,·we·thank·you·all!¶
¶
¶

                             Thank·you,¶

	(Approximately one inch above the end of the page, and between 5.5 and 6" on the horizontal ruler.) Any text you type here will be right aligned automatically.
Type **Ann Salinski**	The text is right aligned.
Close the AutoText toolbar	Choose View, Toolbars, AutoText.
6 Update and close the document	

Topic C: Editing text

This topic covers the following Microsoft Office Specialist exam objectives.

#	Objective
WW03S-1-1	Inserting text, symbols, hidden text and special characters (This objective is also covered in *Word 2003: Intermediate*, in the unit titled "Working with graphics and objects.")
WW03S-1-2	Inserting date and time fields

Editing text in a document

Explanation

Editing a document includes inserting text and applying formats. It might also include deleting unwanted text. To edit text, use the arrow keys or the mouse to move the insertion point.

Inserting text

To insert text, move the insertion point to the place where you want to insert the text, and start typing. As you type, Word inserts the text to the left of the insertion point.

Deleting text

There are several ways to delete text from your documents. The following table shows the different ways:

Press this...	To delete this...
DELETE	One character to the right of the insertion point, without moving the insertion point
← BACKSPACE	One character to the left of the insertion point; also moves the insertion point back one space
CTRL + DELETE	The entire word after the insertion point
CTRL + ← BACKSPACE	The entire word before the insertion point

Do it!

C-1: Inserting and deleting text

Here's how	Here's why
1 Open Plan	
Save the file as **My plan**	In the current unit folder.
Move the mouse over the document area	$\boxed{\text{I}}$
	The pointer changes to an I-beam.
2 In the first paragraph, click as shown	**Executive·Summary** Outlander·Spices·is·a·very small,
	In the first line of the Executive Summary section.
Press (← BACKSPACE)	You've deleted the letter "y" from the word "very."
Press (CTRL) + (← BACKSPACE)	To delete the rest of the word and the extra space between the words "a" and "small."
3 Move to page 3	Use any of the movement options you've learned.
Place the insertion point as shown	¶ **Progress·to·date¶** ¶
	About halfway down the page.
4 Press (CTRL) + (→)	To move to the beginning of the word "to."
Type **Update**	To insert the word "Update" to the left of the word "to."
Press (DELETE) once	To delete the letter "t" from the word "to."
5 Press (CTRL) + (DELETE) twice	To delete the rest of the words in this line.
Update the document	

Overtyping text

Explanation

Sometimes, you might want to replace large blocks of text with new text. You can type the new text and delete the old text, or you can use Overtype mode. When you use *Overtype mode*, the existing text is automatically replaced, character-by-character, by the text you type.

To use Overtype, you must activate this option; it's not active by default. When Overtype mode is active, the Overtype indicator on the status bar is enabled, as shown in Exhibit 2-9. After you've edited the document in Overtype mode, be sure to turn Overtype mode off.

You can turn Overtype on and off by using any of the following methods:

- Choose Tools, Options, and activate or deactivate the Overtype mode check box on the Edit tab.
- Press the Insert key.
- Double-click the Overtype indicator on the status bar.

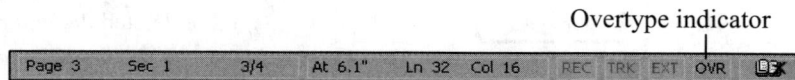

Overtype indicator

| Page 3 | Sec 1 | 3/4 | At 6.1" | Ln 32 | Col 16 | REC | TRK | EXT | OVR | |

Exhibit 2-9: The Overtype indicator on the status bar

Do it!

C-2: Inserting text in different modes

Here's how	Here's why
1 Observe the status bar	Overtype mode is turned off.
2 Choose **Tools, Options...**	The Options dialog box appears.
Click the **Edit** tab	This is where you set editing options.
Verify that the Use the INS key for paste box is clear	☑ Typing replaces selection ☑ Drag-and-drop text editing ☐ Use the INS key for paste ☐ Overtype mode ☑ Use smart cursoring
	Because you will use the Insert key to activate Insert mode, you need to make sure that the Insert key isn't assigned to the paste feature. Overtype mode should not be turned on, or checked, at this time.
3 Click **OK**	
4 Press ⟨INSERT⟩	As indicated in the status bar, Overtype mode is now on.
5 Move to the beginning of page 3	

6 Place the insertion point as shown	• → Control·cash·flow.¶
	
	¶
	In·several·published·studies,
	   1.→ Our·pricing·typicall
	    for·distributors.¶

7 Type **articles**	In the document, "articles" has replaced "studies."
8 Press ⟨INSERT⟩	The Overtype indicator in the status bar is gray now.
9 Type **,**	To insert a comma after the word "articles."
10 Update the document	

Date and time

Explanation

You can insert the current date and time into your document. This can be useful when you're creating memos and reports. You can either leave the date and time as static text or have the date and time automatically updated every time you open or print the document.

To insert the date and time:

1 Place the insertion point where you want to insert the date and time.
2 Choose Insert, Date and Time to open the Date and Time dialog box.
3 From the Available formats box, select a specific date or time format.
4 Check the Update automatically check box if you want the date to be updated automatically in your document. To maintain the date and time as static text, clear this box.
5 Click OK to close the dialog box.

Smart tags

When you insert a date, it's automatically labeled with a smart tag. *Smart tags* identify specific types of information, such as dates, and provide you with a list of related actions, such as scheduling a meeting. A smart tag is indicated by the purple dotted lines that appear beneath text.

By using the smart tag, you can perform actions in Word that would otherwise necessitate opening other programs. For example, you can schedule a meeting by using the smart tag that appears next to a date in the document. To do so, point to the date, click the Smart Tag Actions button, and choose Schedule a Meeting.

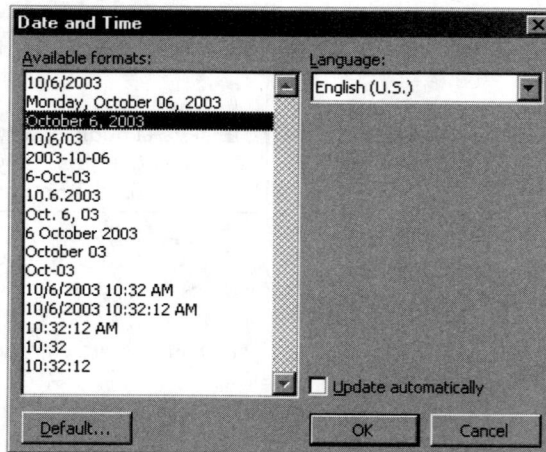

Exhibit 2-10: The Date and Time dialog box

Do it!   **C-3:   Inserting the date and time**

Here's how	Here's why
1 Move to page 1	
Place the insertion point as shown	 Date:¶
Press (SPACEBAR)	
2 Choose **Insert**, **Date and Time...**	To open the Date and Time dialog box. You'll insert the current date and time in the document.
Select the third date format	As shown in Exhibit 2-10.
Verify that the Update automatically box is cleared	To maintain the date and time as static text.
Click **OK**	The current date has been added in the document in the format you chose.
3 Press (↓)	
Observe the date	The purple dotted underline indicates a smart tag.
4 Point to the date as shown	s·Rep⊙rt·for·Pha Date:·October·6,2003¶
	A smart tag appears above the date.
Move the mouse over the smart tag	The smart tag changes to the Smart Tag Actions button.
5 Click as shown	⊙ ▾ t·for·P October·6,·2003¶ Smart Tag Actions
	To display a list of smart tag actions.

6 Observe the menu

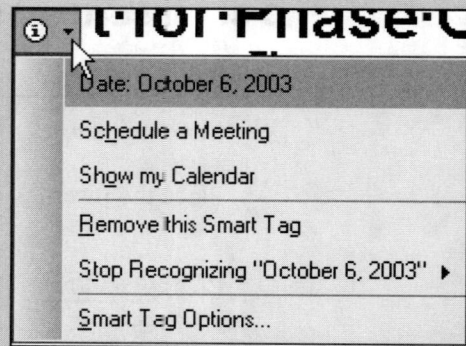

Date: October 6, 2003

Schedule a Meeting

Show my Calendar

Remove this Smart Tag

Stop Recognizing "October 6, 2003" ▶

Smart Tag Options...

It contains commands that can be used to schedule a meeting on that date or to display the calendar. The menu also contains commands to remove the smart tag and to view Smart Tag options.

7 Choose **Show my Calendar**   The Calendar opens in Outlook.

Close the Outlook window

8 Update the document

Topic D: The Undo and Redo commands

Explanation

There might be situations when you need to undo actions, such as entering, deleting, or formatting text. You can do so by using the Undo command. You might also need to repeat your last action, such as formatting text to a specific style or size. You can repeat your last action by using the Redo command.

Using the Undo command

The *Undo* command reverses the most recent action you've performed. You can undo an action in any of three ways:

- Choose Edit, Undo.
- Click the Undo button on the Standard toolbar.
- Press Ctrl+Z.

Undoing multiple actions

You can also undo several actions at once. To do this, click the down arrow next to the Undo button to display a list of the actions. Drag to select the actions that you want to undo from that list; when you release the mouse button, Word will undo *all* of the selected actions. (You can't undo an action without also undoing all the preceding actions in the list.)

Do it!

D-1:   Using the Undo command

Here's how	Here's why
1 Move to the beginning of page 3	
2 Place the insertion point to the left of the word **Project**, as shown	**Project·Justification¶** ¶
3 Press (DELETE) seven times	You've deleted the word "Project."
4 Press (CTRL) + (Z)	To undo the last deletion. The letter "t" is reinserted.
5 Click ↺ ▾	(The Undo button is on the Standard toolbar.) The letter "c" is reinserted.
6 Click the down arrow next to the Undo button	To display the Undo list. You can drag to select the actions you want to undo.
7 Drag to select the five Clear entries, as shown; then click	Clear Clear Clear Clear Clear Date/Time Undo 5 Actions
	To undo your deletions.

Using the Redo command

Explanation

By using the Redo command, you can take back the last action you've undone. You can redo an action in one of three ways:

- Choose Edit, Redo. (The Edit menu shows the Repeat command until you've undone an action; then Repeat changes to Redo.)
- Click the Redo button on the Standard toolbar.
- Press Ctrl+Y.

Redoing multiple actions

In the same manner as the Undo button, the Redo button also contains a list of the actions you've undone. To select multiple actions to redo, drag to select the actions that you want to redo. (Keep in mind that, as with the Undo list, all the actions preceding the last one selected will also be redone.)

Do it!

D-2: Using the Redo command

Here's how	Here's why
1 Click [↻ ▾]	(On the Standard toolbar.) The letter "P" has been deleted.
2 Display the Redo list	Click the down arrow next to the Redo button.
Select the last six actions	Your last six actions are redone. The word "Project" is deleted.
3 Click [↺ ▾] seven times	(Or drag to select the last seven actions.) To reinsert the word "Project" into the document.
4 Update and close the document	

Unit summary: Editing documents

Topic A   In this topic, you learned how to **open** an existing document and **navigate** through it by using scrolling techniques and movement techniques. You moved around in a document by using the scrollbars, the Next Page button, the Previous Page button, and the Select Browse Object button. You used the **Go To command** to move to a specific place in a document. You viewed your document pages by using **Print Layout** and **Reading Layout** views.

Topic B   In this topic, you learned how the **AutoCorrect feature** of Word works. You also added AutoCorrect entries to the AutoCorrect dialog box and used the AutoCorrect Options button. You inserted and created **AutoText** entries. Finally, you learned how to **AutoFormat** a document and how to use the **Click and Type** feature.

Topic C   In this topic, you learned about **editing text**. You inserted and deleted text and used Word's Overtype mode. You also inserted the date in a document by using the Date and Time dialog box. You examined the **date smart tag**.

Topic D   In this topic, you learned how to use the **Undo** and **Redo** commands. You used the toolbar buttons and keyboard shortcuts to undo one action at a time. You also learned how to undo and redo multiple actions at one time.

Independent practice activity

1 Open Celebration and save it as **My celebration**.

2 Insert the current date in the Date field at the beginning of the page.

3 Add an AutoCorrect entry for the word **Outlander**. (*Hint:* Replace **Otulander** with **Outlander**.)

4 Go to the heading "The Project Team" on page 2.

5 Move the insertion point to the left of the P in "Project" and type **Otulander**. (*Hint:* Press the spacebar.)

6 Go to the beginning of page 3.

7 Overwrite the word "Closing" with **Summary**. (*Hint:* Turn off overtype when you're done.)

8 Undo your typing.

9 Update the document and close it.

Review questions

1 How do you use the Undo feature to reverse an action?

2 What navigation technique is the fastest way to move to a specific location in a document?

3 What feature can help you quickly select comments in a document?

4 In which of the following views does the mouse pointer become the Hide White Space tool?

A Normal view

B Print Layout view

C Reading Layout view

D Outline view

5 When inserting text, does the new text appear to the left or right of the insertion point?

6 What is the advantage of using Reading Layout view instead of Print Layout view?

A A better sense of how the document will look when printed

B Ability to hide unwanted toolbars and menus

C Improved readability by automatically scaling text and graphics

D Ability to hide white space

7 When inserted into a document, is the date and time automatically updated to reflect the current date?

8 Which automated feature is used to detect and fix errors, or replace text as you type?

A AutoCorrect

B AutoText

C AutoFormat

D AutoSave

9 How do you turn off the automatic capitalization of the first letter of sentences?

10 What is the difference between the AutoText and AutoFormat features?

11 How is Overtype mode activated?

Unit 3

Moving and copying text

Unit time: 30 minutes

Complete this unit, and you'll know how to:

A Select text by using the mouse and the keyboard.

B Cut, copy, and paste text.

C Search for and replace text.

Topic A: Selecting text

Explanation

When you edit text, you can use the Delete and Backspace keys to delete a single character at a time. To manipulate a larger block of text, you must first select it. *Selecting* text means highlighting it by using the mouse, the keyboard, or a menu command.

After you've selected the text, you can move it or copy it to another location in the document or to another document. You can delete the selected text by pressing Delete or Backspace or by typing new text to replace the selected text. By default, selected text is replaced by anything you type. So, while working with selected text, you need to be careful to avoid accidentally typing over it.

If you select some text, you can also deselect it. To do so, do one of the following:

- Click outside the selected text.
- Select other text.

Using the mouse to select text

There are several ways you can use the mouse to select text. You can drag across the text you want to select, double-click a word to select it, or use a combination of the mouse and the Shift or Ctrl keys. The following table describes various selection techniques:

To...	By...	Do this...
Select a group of words	Dragging	Place your mouse pointer at the beginning of the text you want to select; press and hold the mouse button; and move the pointer across the text. Release the mouse button.
Select a group of words	Using the mouse and (SHIFT)	Place the insertion point at the beginning or end of the text; press and hold the Shift key; and click at the other end of the text.
Select a word	Double-clicking	Place the mouse pointer over the word, and double-click the mouse button.
Select a sentence	Using the mouse and (CTRL)	Place the mouse pointer anywhere in the sentence; press and hold the Ctrl key; and click the mouse button.
Lengthen a selection	Using the mouse and (SHIFT)	Press and hold the Shift key; move the mouse pointer to a new place beyond the current selection; and click the mouse button.
Shorten a selection	Using the mouse and (SHIFT)	Press and hold the Shift key; move the mouse pointer to a new place inside the current selection; and click the mouse button.

Outlander Spices understands that the wholesale distributors who will thrive in today's marketplace are those who can do the following four things:¶

- → Keep inventory costs and levels under control¶
- → Provide high-quality products¶
- → Price products competitively¶
- → Control cash flow¶

¶

In several published studies, our product lines have consistently outperformed other brands in three ways:¶

1. → Our pricing typically undercuts that of our competitors, yet still provides a large margin of profit for distributors.¶
2. → Our products are manufactured for quality and have earned end-user loyalty, which has resulted in repeat sales.¶
3. → Our products move! Inventory typically turns over 50% faster than competitive products do, and this increases freshness and shelf life.¶

Exhibit 3-1: Selected text in a document appears highlighted

Do it!

A-1:   Using the mouse to select text

Here's how	Here's why
1 Open Expansion	
Save the document as **My expansion**	
Move to the upper part of page 3	
2 Double-click **Justification**	To select the word.

3 Place the insertion point as shown	In·several·published·studies,·
	    1.·→·Our·pricing·typically
	       for·distributors.¶

4 Drag the mouse to the end of the word **competitors**	To select the text you dragged across, as shown in Exhibit 3-1.
5 Click outside the selection	To deselect the text.
6 Place the insertion point as shown	¶ Our·customers·have·saved restaurants·throughout·the At the beginning of the paragraph that follows the numbered list.
7 Press and hold `CTRL`	
8 Click the sentence	To select the sentence, including the punctuation and the trailing space at the end.
Release `CTRL`	
9 Move to the top of page 1	
10 Select the word **Expansion**	Double-click the word in the heading on page 1.
11 Deselect the text	Click outside the selection.
Update the document	

Using the keyboard to select text

Explanation

You can use the arrow keys, the Home and End keys, and the Shift key to select text or other elements, such as graphics, in your documents.

The following table explains how to use the keyboard to select text:

Key	Action
SHIFT + ←	Selects the text to the left of the insertion point one character at a time
SHIFT + →	Selects the text to the right of the insertion point one character at a time
SHIFT + ↑	Selects text from the left of the insertion point to the same place in the previous line
SHIFT + ↓	Selects text from the right of the insertion point to the same place in the next line
SHIFT + HOME	Selects text from the left of the insertion point to the beginning of the current line
SHIFT + END	Selects text from the right of the insertion point to the end of the current line

Do it!

A-2: Using the keyboard to select text

Here's how	Here's why
1 Move to the beginning of the first paragraph on page 2	It begins with "The Expansion Project team."
Place the insertion point as shown	**The·Project·Team¶** ¶ The·Expansion·Project·team·is·currently·of·internal·and·external·people·provides·
2 Press and hold SHIFT	
3 Press → three times	To select the word "The."
4 Press END	To select the first line of the paragraph.
5 Press ↓ three times	To select the entire paragraph.
Release SHIFT	
Deselect the paragraph	Click anywhere in the document.

Using the selection bar to select text

Explanation

Word also has an area called the *selection bar* that's useful for selecting lines, paragraphs, or an entire document. The selection bar is located on the left side of the document window. You'll know when you're in the selection bar because the mouse pointer will change to a right-pointing arrow.

The following table describes techniques for using the selection bar:

To...	By...	Do this...
Select a line	Using the selection bar	From the selection bar, point to the line you want to select, and click the mouse button.
Select multiple lines	Using the selection bar	Point to the first or last line of text you want to select; press and hold the mouse button; drag down or up to the last line of text; then release the mouse button.
Select a paragraph	Using the selection bar	Point to the paragraph from the selection bar, and double-click the mouse button.
Select the entire document	Using the selection bar and CTRL	Point to any line of the document; press and hold the CTRL key; and click the mouse button. You can also choose Edit, Select All.

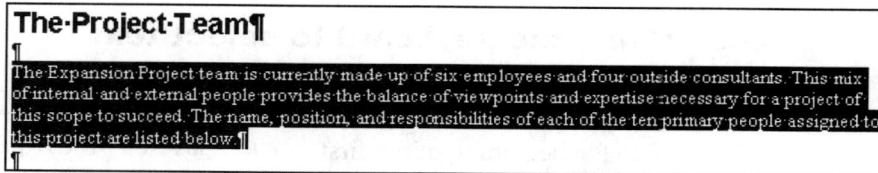

The·Project·Team¶

The·Expansion·Project·team·is·currently·made·up·of·six·employees·and·four·outside·consultants.·This·mix·of·internal·and·external·people·provides·the·balance·of·viewpoints·and·expertise·necessary·for·a·project·of·this·scope·to·succeed.·The·name,·position,·and·responsibilities·of·each·of·the·ten·primary·people·assigned·to·this·project·are·listed·below.¶

Exhibit 3-2: The entire paragraph selected by using the selection bar

Do it!

A-3:   Using the selection bar to select text

Here's how	Here's why
1 Move the pointer to the far left side of the screen	When the pointer is in the selection bar, it becomes a right-pointing arrow.
2 From the selection bar, point to the first line of the last paragraph on page 1	It begins with "In the following report." The mouse pointer should be a right-pointing arrow.
Click the mouse button	To select the first line of the paragraph.

3	Point to the first paragraph of page 2	From the selection bar.
	Double-click the mouse button	To select the paragraph, as shown in Exhibit 3-2.
	Deselect the text	
4	Select the first line of the first paragraph on page 2	Click at the beginning of the first line, and drag across the line.
5	Press and hold (SHIFT)	
	Click after the word **scope**	To extend your selection. If you used the selection bar in the previous step, the entire third line will be selected now.
	Release (SHIFT)	
	Deselect the text	
6	Press and hold (CTRL)	
	Click the selection bar	To select the entire document.
	Release (CTRL)	
7	Type **a**	The entire document has been replaced with the letter "a."
8	Undo your typing	Click the Undo button, or choose Edit, Undo Typing.
9	Deselect the selection	
	Update the document	

Topic B: Cutting, copying, and pasting text

This topic covers the following Microsoft Office Specialist exam objective.

#	Objective
WW03S-1-1	Deleting, cutting, copying, pasting text and using the clipboard

Cutting and pasting text

Explanation

In Word, you can move and copy text from one place in a document to another location, in the same document or another document. This saves hours of retyping and ensures consistency within or among documents.

You can move a block of text by using the Cut and Paste commands. The text will be inserted in the new location, to the left of the insertion point. To move text in a document or between documents:

1   Select the text you want to move.
2   Click the Cut button on the Standard toolbar, press Ctrl+X, or choose Edit, Cut.
3   Place the insertion point in the new location.
4   Click the Paste button, press Ctrl+V, or choose Edit, Paste.

The Office Clipboard

When you cut or copy text, Word places the selected text on the Office Clipboard. The *Office Clipboard* is a temporary storage area that holds the text for you to specify where to place it. The Office Clipboard appears in the Clipboard task pane. The Office Clipboard can hold up to 24 items. The collected items stay on the Clipboard until you close the Office application.

You can display the Clipboard task pane by choosing Edit, Office Clipboard. By default, the Clipboard is empty. As items are cut or copied from the document, they'll appear in the Office Clipboard gallery. The most recent item is listed at the top of the gallery. From this task pane, you can paste or delete a single item or all of the items.

To paste a single item, position the insertion point in the desired location and click the entry in the gallery. You can also click the drop-down arrow next to the Clipboard item and choose Paste. To paste all of the Clipboard items, click the Paste All button.

To delete a single item, click the drop-down arrow and choose Delete. To delete all of the Clipboard items, click Clear All.

The Paste Options button

After you paste text, the Paste Options button appears to the right of the pasted text. You can use this button to specify the formatting of the pasted information. For example, you can choose to keep the text formatting as it is or inherit the formatting of the destination paragraph. To use the Paste Options button, click the down arrow and select the relevant formatting option.

Do it!   ## B-1:   Moving text and using Paste Options

Here's how	Here's why
1 Choose **Edit, Office Clipboard...**	To display the Clipboard task pane. Anything you cut or copy from the document will appear in this gallery.
2 Move to page 2	
3 Select **Kathy Sinclair, Project Management Consultant** and the paragraph underneath	Use the selection bar or drag over the text.
Click ✂	(The Cut button is on the Standard toolbar.) To place the text on the Clipboard. Ann Salinski, VP Financial Services, is now the first team member. Notice that the cut text appears in the Clipboard task pane.
4 Click as shown	creation·of·a·training·initiative·and·do〈 |**Thomas·Boorman,·IT·Consultant**¶ Thomas·will·build·the·initial·Web·site,
	The team member under Kim Leong. You'll paste the text that was cut.
Click 📋	(The Paste button is on the Standard toolbar.) To paste the text above the insertion point.
5 Observe the Paste Options button	**Thomas·Boorman,·IT·Consu[📋]nt**¶ Thomas·will·build·the·initial·Web·site,
	The text has been pasted above the insertion point, and the Paste Options button appears below the pasted selection.
Click the Paste Options button	📋▾ ·site·train·an·internal·person· ⦿ Keep Source Formatting ○ Match Destination Formatting ○ Keep Text Only 44 Apply Style or Formatting...
	A list of options appears. By using this list, you can specify how to handle the formatting for the newly pasted text. By default, the Keep Source Formatting option is selected. You can remove all formatting by selecting the Keep Text Only option.
Select **Keep Text Only**	Notice that all the formatting is lost from the pasted text.

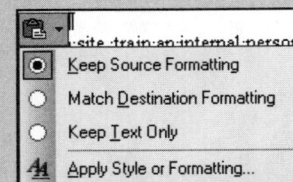

6 From the Paste Options list, select **Keep Source Formatting**	To retain the source formatting of the text.
7 Update the document	

Copying text

Explanation

There are times when you might want to use a block of text again in the same document or in another document. You can do this by copying the text to the Clipboard and pasting it in the new location. To copy text, you use the Copy and Paste commands. Copied text is insert to the left of the insertion point.

To copy text:

1 Select the text you want to copy.

2 Click the Copy button on the Standard toolbar, press Ctrl+C, or choose Edit, Copy.

3 Place the insertion point in the new location.

4 Paste the text.

Do it!

B-2: Copying text in a document

Here's how	Here's why
1 Move to the beginning of page 1	
2 Select the title	Outlander Spices Expansion Project Progress Report for Phase One.
Click [icon]	(The Copy button is on the Standard Toolbar.) To copy the text to the Clipboard. The text appears at the top of the list in the Clipboard task pane. The heading text is still visible because you copied the text instead of cutting it.
3 Move to the top of page 4	
Place the insertion point as shown	¶ successful implementation.¶ ¶ **Outstanding·Issues·for·Phase·One¶** ¶ The·following·issues·are·still·outstanding·as·of·this·report:¶
Click [icon]	The heading is now at the top of page 4, and the Paste Options button appears below it.
4 Update the document	

Copying text between documents

Explanation

There will be times when you want to copy text from one document to another. For example, you might want to copy some text from a long report into a memo or copy a return address into multiple letters.

To copy text between documents, you use the same process that you use to copy text within a document.

Do it!

B-3: Copying text from one document to another

Here's how	Here's why
1 Select all the text on page 4	From the heading, "Outlander Spices Expansion Project Progress Report for Phase One," onward.
Copy the text to the Clipboard	Click the Copy button.
2 Click	To create a blank document. The Clipboard task pane isn't displayed in the new document.
Paste the text into the new document	(Click the Paste button.) The selected text has been copied into the new document.
3 Save the new document as **My issue**	(In the current unit folder.) Choose File, Save As, or click the Save button; type the file name in the File name box; and click Save.
4 Close the new document	Choose File, Close.
5 Deselect the text	In My expansion, click outside the selection.
Click **Clear All**	(The Clear All button is in the Clipboard task pane.) To delete all Clipboard items.
6 Close the Clipboard task pane	Click the Close button in the upper-right corner of the task pane.
Update the document	

Topic C: Finding and replacing text

This topic covers the following Microsoft Office Specialist exam objective.

#	Objective
WW03S-1-3	Finding and replacing text

Finding text

Explanation

When you're working in a long document, it can be time-consuming to find a specific word or words. For example, you might want to find a paragraph of text that contains the word "project," but are not sure which page contains the paragraph. Word provides a Find command to help you find specific text. You can also replace text in a document by using the Replace command.

To use the Find command, you use the Find and Replace dialog box, and you enter the word or words you want to search for. By default, Word searches the entire document beginning from the insertion point and going downward from there. If you start the search from the middle of a document, however, Word goes back to the beginning of the document and continues searching until it reaches the insertion point.

Refining your search

You can refine your search by using additional options in the Find and Replace dialog box. When you find a word for the first time, these options are hidden. To see them, click More. A list of options appears in the dialog box. You can use them alone or in combination to search your document. For example, if you choose the option "Match case," and you type the word "Project," Word will find only those instances of the word "Project" that begin with an uppercase "P." If you choose "Find whole words only" and type the word "Project," Word will find each instance of "project" in either upper- or lowercase, but will not find "projects" because your search criteria did not include an "s."

To use the Find command to search for text in a document:

1   Choose Edit, Find or press Ctrl+F to open the Find and Replace dialog box.

2   In the Find what box, enter the text you want to find.

3   Click More, and select any search criteria you want to use to refine the search. You can click Less to hide the additional search options and reduce the size of the dialog box.

4   Click Find Next until you've found what you're looking for.

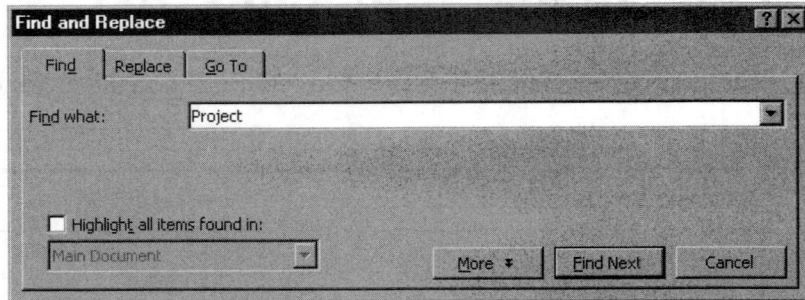

Exhibit 3-3: The Find tab in the Find and Replace dialog box

Do it!

C-1:   Searching for a word

Here's how	Here's why
1 Move to the beginning of page 1	In My expansion.
2 Choose **Edit, Find…**	The Find and Replace dialog box appears. The Find tab is active.
In the Find what box, enter **Project**	As shown in Exhibit 3-3.
Click **Find Next**	To search for the first occurrence of the word "project."
3 Move the dialog box to the left and observe the screen	(Drag the dialog box by its title bar.) Word found "Project" in the heading on page 1.
4 Click **Find Next**	Word finds the next occurrence of the word "project." This time it's lowercase.
5 Click **More**	To see additional search options. Notice that the button changes to Less.
Under Search Options, check **Match case**	
	In the list of search options.
Click **Less**	To hide the Search Options and reduce the size of the dialog box.
6 Click **Find Next**	This time the word "project" is capitalized.

7 Click **Find Next** until you reach the end of the document	To continue searching for all occurrences of the word "Project" with an uppercase "P."

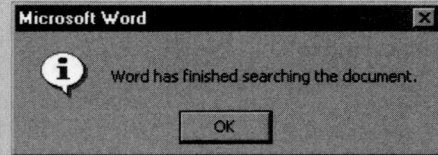

Microsoft Word	☒
(i) Word has finished searching the document.	
OK	

A message box appears, indicating that Word has finished searching the document.

Click **OK**	To close the message box.
8 Click **Cancel**	To close the Find and Replace dialog box.

Replacing text

Explanation

There might be situations when you want to replace several instances of a word or phrase with a different word or phrase. To do this, you can use the Replace command in Word. The Replace command is actually an extension of the Find command. On the Replace tab of the Find and Replace dialog box, you enter the word that will be replaced and the word you want to replace it with.

When you find the first occurrence of the text, you can use the Replace button to replace a single occurrence. Or you can use the Replace All button to replace all occurrences in one step and bypass further prompts. However, be careful when using this option because you could replace an occurrence of the word when you don't really want to.

To replace text in a document:

1 Choose Edit, Replace to open the Find and Replace dialog box with the Replace tab active.

2 In the Find what box, type the text you're replacing.

3 In the Replace with box, type the text you're substituting.

4 Click More to specify additional search options, such as matching case or finding whole words.

5 Click Find Next.

6 Click Replace to replace the text one occurrence at a time, or click Replace All to replace all occurrences at the same time.

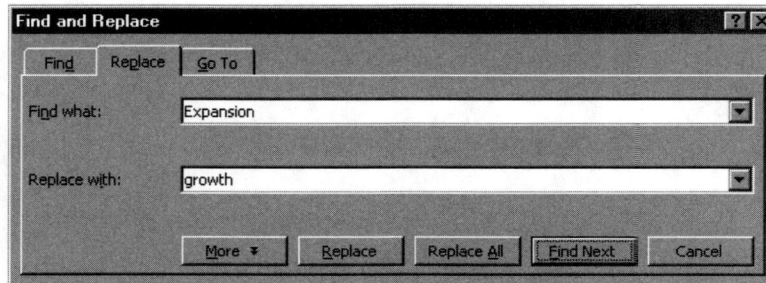

Exhibit 3-4: Using the Replace tab

Do it!

C-2: Replacing text in a document

Here's how	Here's why
1 Move to the beginning of the document	(If necessary.) It's easier to begin a search and replace from the beginning of the document.
2 Choose **Edit, Replace...**	(To open the Find and Replace dialog box as shown in Exhibit 3-4.) The Replace tab is activated. You use this dialog box to search for and replace text.
3 Edit the Find what box to read **Expansion**	The Match case option remains selected because it was checked in the most recent find.
Press ⌷TAB⌷	To move to the Replace with box.
4 In the Replace with box, enter **growth**	You'll replace "Expansion" with "growth."
5 Clear **Match case**	If necessary, click More to display the Search options.
Click **Less**	
6 Click **Find Next**	Word found the word "Expansion" in the heading. You might need to drag the dialog box out of the way to see the highlighted text.
7 Click **Replace**	To replace this occurrence of "expansion." Word finds the next occurrence of "Expansion."
8 Click **Find Next**	To skip this occurrence of "expansion" and leave it intact.
9 Click **Replace**	To replace the next occurrence of "Expansion."
Skip the next replacement	Click Find Next.
10 Replace any remaining occurrences of "expansion"	Click Replace to confirm each one. At the end, a message box appears, stating that "Word has finished searching the document."
11 Click **OK**	To confirm that Word has completed the search.
12 Close the dialog box	
Update and close the document	

Unit summary: Moving and copying text

Topic A   In this topic, you learned how to use the mouse and the keyboard to **select text**. You also used the **selection bar** to select lines, paragraphs, and the entire document.

Topic B   In this topic, you learned how to **move** and **copy** text in a document. You also used the Paste Options button to specify the formatting of pasted information. In addition, you copied text between documents.

Topic C   In this topic, you learned how to search for text by using the **Find and Replace** dialog box. You also examined search options such as matching case. You learned how to replace the found text by using the Replace tab in the Find and Replace dialog box.

Independent practice activity

1 Open Memo from the current unit folder.

2 Save it as **My memo.**

3 Select the heading "The Project Team" and related text up to the heading "To-do list."

4 Cut your selection.

5 Paste it at the end of the document.

6 Search for the word **Define** in the complete document, and replace it with **Identify**. Then close the Find and Replace dialog box. (*Hint:* Match the case.)

7 Update and close the document.

Review questions

1 What are the three basic text selection methods introduced in this course?

2 What is the first step when deleting, cutting, or copying text?

3 Which of the following is the temporary storage area that holds text until you specify where to place it?

   A Cache

   B Word's temp folder

   C The task pane

   D Office Clipboard

4 Is it possible to view the contents of the Office Clipboard? If so, how?

5 What is the difference between cutting text and copying text?

6 What are the steps for finding specific text in a document?

7 How can you verify that your client's name is spelled correctly in the document?

8 Select the best description of the Replace command.

   A Enables you to search a document for a specific word.

   B Enables you to correct a misspelled word in a document.

   C Enables you to search a document for specific text and replace it with different text.

   D Enables you to search a document for edited text and accept the changes.

Unit 4

Formatting characters and paragraphs

Unit time: 90 minutes

Complete this unit, and you'll know how to:

A Change the appearance of text by applying character formatting.

B Align text by using tabs.

C Format paragraphs by aligning text, adding borders, and applying bullets and numbering.

D Change paragraph indents, line spacing, and paragraph spacing.

Topic A: Character formatting

This topic covers the following Microsoft Office Specialist exam objectives.

#	Objective
WW03S-3-1	Finding and modifying font typeface, style, color and size
WW03S-3-1	Applying highlights to text
WW03S-3-1	Applying text effects
WW03S-3-1	Modifying character spacing
WW03S-5-7	Revealing formatting and hidden text (This objective is also covered in the unit titled "Getting started.")
WW03E-5-3	Modifying default font settings

Character formats

Explanation

You can use character formats to improve the appearance of your documents. *Character formats* include fonts, font styles, and font sizes. You can draw a reader's attention to parts of a document and improve its readability by applying character formatting.

You can apply character formatting to text by using the various options in the Font dialog box or by using the buttons on the Formatting toolbar.

When you use character formatting, avoid using too many different kinds. Using too much character formatting can make your document difficult to read. Keep in mind that the purpose of character formatting is to draw attention to important parts of the text.

Font styles

Font styles (also called *type styles*) include bold, italic, and underline. You can emphasize a specific word or words by using these styles. For example, using a bold format to highlight a heading, such as the heading you see in this course book, helps draw a reader's attention to important information and sections in the document.

Fonts and font sizes

Changing the font and size of text is another way to draw attention to important information. The design of the characters is called a *font* (or a *typeface*). Two commonly used fonts are Times New Roman and Arial. Two categories of fonts are serif and sans serif.

A *serif* font has small lines at the top and bottom of letters. (Think of them as small feet at the bottom of the letters.) For example, the font used in this paragraph, Times New Roman, is a serif font. A serif font works well on a printed page with large blocks of text because the lines lead the eye across the page.

A *sans serif* font lacks the small lines of a serif font. For example, the font in the heading at the beginning of this page is a sans serif font. A sans serif font works well for headings because the lack of lines at the top and base of the letters makes the text stand out.

The Formatting toolbar

The easiest way to apply font styles to text is to select the text and use the Bold, Italic, or Underline buttons on the Formatting toolbar. You can also apply these font styles by using the keyboard. The following table shows the font styles and the buttons and keys used to apply them:

Style	Button	Keyboard
Bold	**B**	CTRL + B
Italic	*I*	CTRL + I
Underline	U	CTRL + U

Removing font styles

There might be times when you want to remove any extra formatting and return the text to the underlying style. To remove all the character formatting from text, select the text and press Ctrl+Spacebar.

Do it!

A-1: Using the Formatting toolbar

Here's how	Here's why
1 Open Project	(From the current unit folder.) You'll improve the formatting in this document.
Save the document as **My project**	In the current unit folder.
2 Move to page 4	
Select **Thomas Boorman, IT Consultant**	The eighth person in the project team list.
3 Click **B**	The Bold button is on the Formatting toolbar.
Deselect the text, and observe the screen	You've applied a bold style to the text.
4 Move to page 5	
Select as shown	·over·**50%·faster**·than·
	In the first line of the third item in the numbered list.
5 Click *I*	The Italic button is on the Formatting toolbar.
Deselect the text	The text is italic.
6 Select **50% faster**	
Press CTRL + SPACEBAR	The formatting has been removed.
7 Click *I*	To reapply the italic format.
8 Select **14%**	In the next paragraph on the same page.
Press CTRL + I	To italicize the text. You can also use the Italic button.
Italicize **132%**	In the next paragraph on page 5.
9 Update the document	

The Font dialog box

Explanation

You can also use the Font dialog box to apply character formats. When applying multiple character formats, you can apply them all by using the dialog box instead of by using the various buttons and lists on the Formatting toolbar. The Font dialog box also offers several additional options for applying character formats, such as font color, underline style, underline color, and text effects.

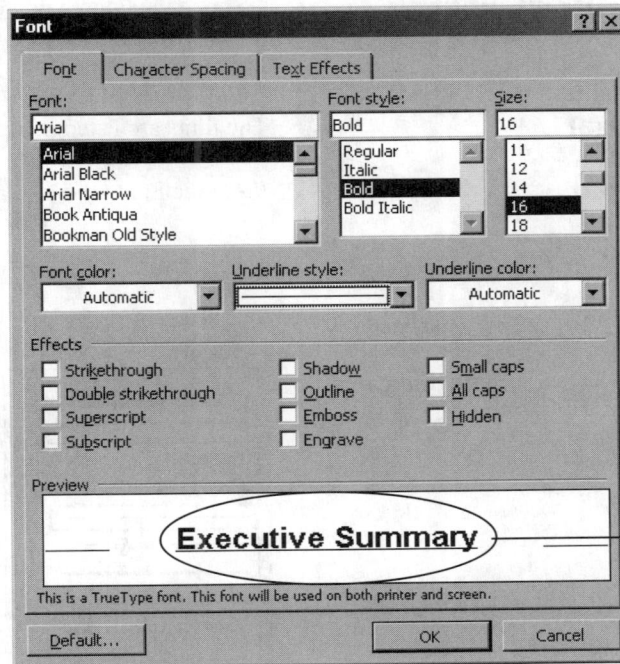

Preview of formatting applied to the text

Exhibit 4-1: The preview of text in the Font dialog box

Do it!   **A-2:   Using the Font dialog box**

Here's how	Here's why
1 Move to the beginning of page 3	
Select **Executive Summary**	
2 Choose **Format**, **Font...**	To open the Font dialog box. You'll see options for choosing a font, font style, and font size, as well as other options.
3 Select **Arial**	The fonts are listed in alphabetical order.
Select **Bold**	From the Font style list.
Select **16**	From the Size list.
4 Display the Underline style list	You'll see different styles for underlines.
From the list, select the indicated line	
Observe the Preview pane	(Near the lower region of the dialog box.) The preview of how the text will look with this formatting applied appears, as shown in Exhibit 4-1.
Click **OK**	To apply the formatting you've chosen.
5 Deselect the text	You've applied several character formats to the text at once.
6 Update the document	

Character effects

Explanation Among the formatting options available in the Font dialog box are character effects, such as superscript, subscript, small caps, shadow, and hidden text. These effects can be used for creating certain phrases, such as A^+, H_2O, or A^2.

Text effects

You can use the Text Effects tab in the Font dialog box to apply text animations. For example, you can choose to have a flashing outline surround your text.

Character spacing

You can use the Character Spacing tab in the Font dialog box to modify the amount of space between letters in the selected text.

To apply character effects to text:

1 Select the word or phrase you want to format.
2 Choose Format, Font to open the Font dialog box.
3 In the Effects section, check the options you want to apply.
4 Use the Text Effects tab to apply animations to text.
5 Use the Character Spacing tab to modify the space between letters.
6 Click OK.

Do it!

A-3: Applying character and text effects

Here's how	Here's why
1 Move to page 1	
Place the insertion point as shown	Outlander·Spices|
2 Type **TM**	You want to display this text as the trademark symbol with the superscript effect.
Select **TM**	
3 Choose **Format, Font...**	To open the Font dialog box.
Under Effects, check **Superscript**	
Click **OK**	The text "TM" now appears slightly higher than the company name "Outlander Spices."
4 On page 2, select **Table of Contents**	Table of Contents

5 Open the Font dialog box	Choose Format, Font, or press Ctrl+D.
Click the **Character Spacing** tab	
In the Spacing list, select **Expanded**	Spacing: [Expanded ▼]
	To increase the amount of space between the letters of "Table of Contents."
Edit the By box to read **5** pt	By: [5]pt [▲▼]
Click **OK**	**Table of Contents**
6 Move to page 5	
Select text as shown	We·have·also·experienced·a·*132%*·growth·in·West·Coast.·This·success·and·current·market·
	You'll apply a text effect to the percentage-growth figure.
7 Open the Font dialog box	
Click the **Text Effects** tab	
From the Animations list, select **Marching Black Ants**	Animations: (none) Blinking Background Las Vegas Lights Marching Black Ants Marching Red Ants Shimmer Sparkle Text
	The Preview pane displays a sample of the animation.
Click **OK**	
8 Deselect and observe the text	experienced·a·*132%*·growth·his·success·and·current·mark
	The text animation has been applied to the text.
9 Update the document	

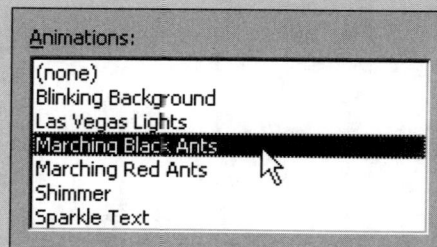

Using the Highlight tool

Explanation

You can draw attention to specific text by marking it with a different color. You can do this by clicking the down arrow next to the Highlight button on the Formatting toolbar and selecting a color.

There are two ways to use this tool:

- One-time use:
    1. Select the text you want to highlight.
    2. Click the Highlight button. The highlight is applied, and the tool is turned off automatically.
- Multiple use:
    1. Click the Highlight button.
    2. Select the text you want to highlight.
    3. Continue to select text to highlight. The tool remains active until you click the Highlight button again to turn it off.

Do it!

A-4: Highlighting text

Here's how	**Here's why**
1 Move to page 4	
Select **Susan Gianni, Business Consultant**	(The last person in the project team list.) You'll highlight the selected text.
2 Click the arrow next to the Highlight button, as shown	The Highlight button is on the Formatting toolbar. A ToolTip with the Highlight button states the default color.
3 Select bright green as shown	To highlight the text in bright green. This green color will remain on the Highlight button until you choose a different color.
4 Update the document	

Repeating character formatting

Explanation

At times, you might want to repeat certain character formatting in several parts of a document. You can use Word's Repeat command to apply the same formatting to other selected text within a document. This option is especially useful when you're using the Font dialog box because you can apply all the formats at the same time and then repeat the formatting throughout the document.

To repeat font formatting that you've just applied, you can choose Edit, Repeat Font Formatting, or press F4, which is the Repeat shortcut key.

Do it!

A-5: Repeating formatting in a document

Here's how	Here's why
1 Move to the beginning of page 4	
Select **The Project Team**	
2 Open the Font dialog box	
Click the **Font** tab	
Apply **Arial**, **Bold**, **14** formatting	To change the font, font style, and font size.
Click **OK**	To apply the formatting to the text you selected.
3 Move to page 5	
Select **Progress Update**	The paragraph above the bulleted list, about two-thirds of the way down the page.
4 Choose **Edit, Repeat Font Formatting**	To apply the same formatting to this text.
5 Move to the beginning of page 6	
Select **Outstanding issues for Phase One**	Near the beginning of the page.
6 Press F4	To repeat the formatting.
7 Deselect the text	
Update the document	

Formatting multiple selections

Explanation

While formatting, you can easily select multiple areas in a document at the same time. This saves time because you don't have to repeat the formatting again. For example, you might want to format all headings in the document in a similar manner. All you need to do is select a heading, press Ctrl, and select the next heading. After selecting all the headings, you can format them at the same time.

You can also use the Find feature to simultaneously select formatted text and reformat it. To do so, open the Find and Replace dialog box, and leave the Find what and Replace with boxes empty. Click the Format button as shown in Exhibit 4-2, and choose Font from the menu. Specify the formatting options you want to search for, and click OK to close the Font dialog box. When you click the Find All button, Word finds and highlights all occurrences of the specified format.

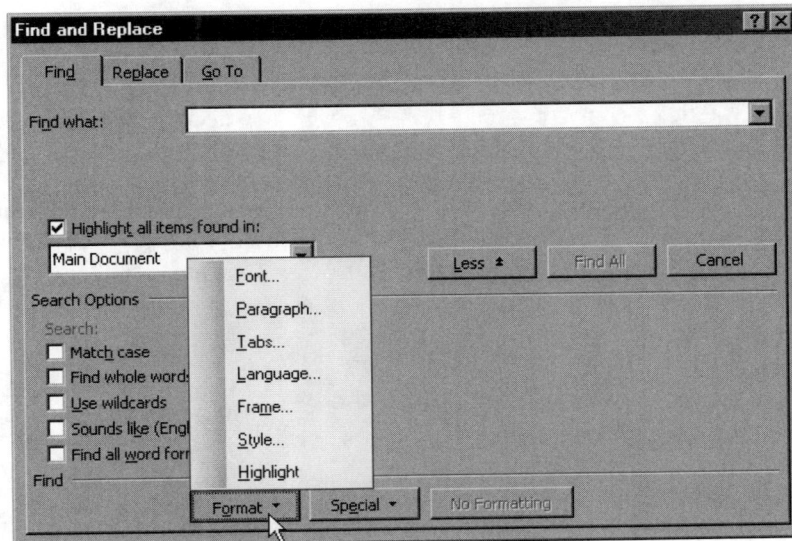

Exhibit 4-2: The Format menu in the Find and Replace dialog box

Do it!

A-6: Formatting multiple selections simultaneously

	Here's how	Here's why
1	Choose **Edit**, **Find...**	To open the Find and Replace dialog box.
	Delete the selected text in the Find what box	If necessary.
2	Check **Highlight all items found in:**	To make multiple selections in the document.
	Verify that **Main Document** is selected from the list	
	Click **More**	(If necessary.) To view all the options in the Find and Replace dialog box.
3	Click **Format**	To display the Format menu, as shown in Exhibit 4-2.
	Choose **Font...**	To open the Find Font dialog box.
	On the Font tab, apply **Arial**, **Bold**, **14** formatting	To apply font, font style, and font size.
	Click **OK**	
4	Click **Less**	(In the Find and Replace dialog box.) To hide the search options.
5	Click **Find All**	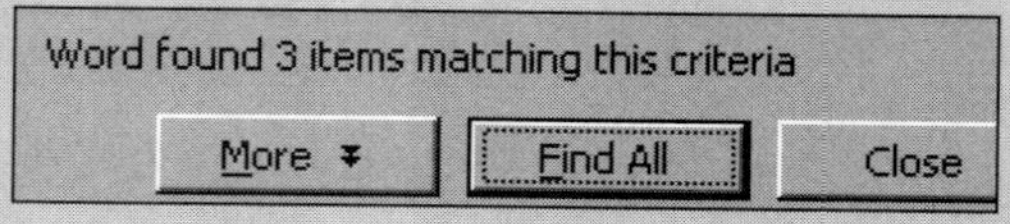Word found 3 items matching this criteria More Find All Close To find all occurrences of the specified format. A message appears above the Find All button, telling you that Word found three items.
	Click **Close**	All three headings are now highlighted.

6 Open the Font dialog box

Select the indicated underline style

Underline style:

(none)

(none)
Words only

Click **OK**

Deselect the headings   To see that they are underlined.

7 Update the document

Using the Format Painter to apply character formatting

Explanation

Word provides another option, the Format Painter, for repeating formatting in a document. The *Format Painter* is a button, on the Standard toolbar, that copies the formatting of text and applies it to other text you select. This tool can save time if you're working with a document that you've already partially formatted. For example, if you like the format of a heading, you can use the Format Painter to copy the format to all other headings in the document.

To repeat formatting by using the Format Painter:

1   Select the text whose format you want to copy.
2   Click the Format Painter.
3   Select the text to be formatted.

Do it!

A-7:   Using the Format Painter

Here's how	Here's why
1 Move to the beginning of page 4	If necessary.
Select **Ann Salinski, VP Financial Services**	The first person in the project team list.
2 Click [icon]	(The Format Painter button is on the Standard toolbar.) To copy the format of the text.
3 Select **Jack Thomas, VP Sales**	To apply the formatting to this text.
4 Click [icon]	To copy the newly applied format.
Apply the format to **Elise Sechan, Manager, Information Technologies**	Drag the Format Painter tool over the Elise's name and title to apply the formatting.
5 Update the document	

The Reveal Formatting task pane

Explanation

The Reveal Formatting task pane shows information related to the formatting in your document. This pane displays the current font and paragraph formatting of the selected text.

To open the Reveal Formatting task pane, choose Format, Reveal Formatting. Select the text whose formatting information you want to view. For example, in Exhibit 4-3, the heading "Outlander Spices" appears in the Selected text box. The applied formatting is displayed in the task pane. Exhibit 4-3 shows you that the heading's font format is Arial, 24 pt, bold. You can click the blue text to open the Font dialog box and change the formatting.

From the Reveal Formatting task pane, you can also apply the formatting of the surrounding text to the selected text. To do this, click the arrow in the Selected text box, and select Apply Formatting of Surrounding text. To remove formatting from the selected text, choose Clear Formatting.

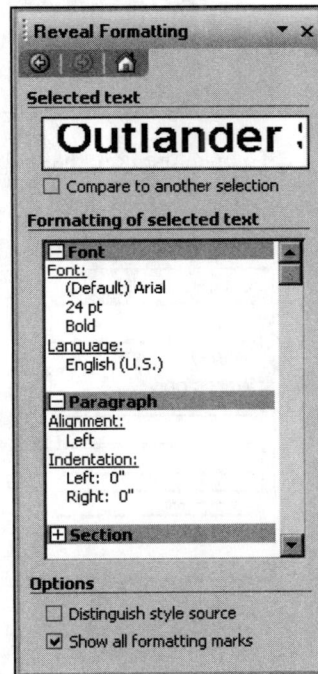

Exhibit 4-3: The Reveal Formatting task pane

Comparing formatting

You can also compare the text formatting in a document. Verify that the desired text appears in the Selected text box. Then, check Compare to another selection, and a second Selected text box appears. Finally, select the text to be compared. The result of the comparison is shown in the Formatting differences box.

A-8: Using the Reveal Formatting task pane

Here's how	Here's why
1 Choose **Format**, **Reveal Formatting…**	To open the Reveal Formatting task pane, which displays the formatting of the selected text, "Elise Sechan, Manager, Information Technologies." The font, language, alignment, indentation, and spacing options appear.
2 Move to page 1	
Select the heading	The formatting of the selected heading appears in the Reveal Formatting task pane, as shown in Exhibit 4-3.
3 In the Reveal Formatting task pane, click **Font** as shown	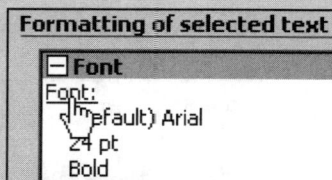

Formatting of selected text

☐ **Font**
Font:
(Default) Arial
24 pt
Bold |
| | To open the Font dialog box. |
| From the Size list, select **26** | |
| 4 From the Underline style list, select as shown |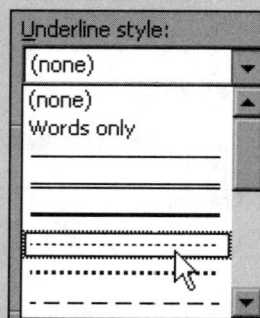

Underline style:
(none)
(none)
Words only |
Click **OK**	
Deselect the heading	The size of the heading has increased, and a dotted line appears below it.
5 Move to page 4	
Select **Ron Timmons, Senior Buyer**	The formatting of this text is different from that of the other team members' names. You'll find out the differences in formatting and restore the formatting accordingly.
6 Check **Compare to another selection**	(In the Reveal Formatting task pane.) You'll compare the formatting of "Ron Timmons" to "Aileen MacElvoy."
7 Select **Aileen MacElvoy, Director of Marketing**	(In the document above the team member Ron Timmons.) This is the second section of text.

8 Observe the Formatting differences box

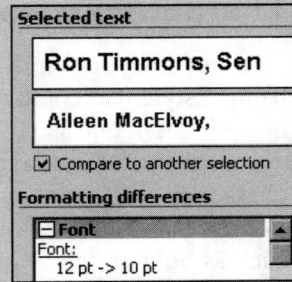

Selected text

Ron Timmons, Sen

Aileen MacElvoy,

☑ Compare to another selection

Formatting differences

⊟ Font
Font:
    12 pt -> 10 pt

The differences in the two sections of text appear in the box. The first selection has a font size of 12 pt; the second selection has a font size of 10 pt.

Clear **Compare to another selection**

9 Select **Ron Timmons, Senior Buyer**

Change the font to 10 pt

(Click Font in the Reveal Formatting task pane, and select 10 pt from the Size list.) The formatting of this text now matches the other names.

10 Move to page 1

Select the heading

11 In the task pane, display the Selected text list

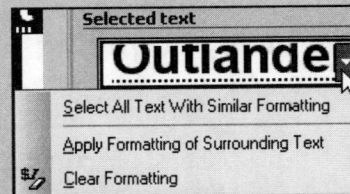

Selected text

Outlande

Select All Text With Similar Formatting

Apply Formatting of Surrounding Text

Clear Formatting

From the list, select **Clear Formatting**

All the formatting has been removed, and the text appears with the default format.

12 Click ↶ ▾

To undo the clear action and reapply the formatting.

13 Use the task pane to remove the underline from the heading

Click Font, and specify none in the Underline style list.

14 Close the Reveal Formatting task pane

Deselect the text

If necessary.

15 Update the document

Character styles

Explanation

You can apply multiple formats to text either by selecting the formats individually or by using a style that contains the formats. A *style* is a collection of various formats that can be applied, in one step, to paragraphs, characters, or tables. A paragraph style affects the appearance of the paragraph, such as its alignment, line spacing, and tab settings. A character style affects the font, size, or font style of selected text. (Don't confuse a Word style—a named collection of formats, such as "Heading 1"—with a font style, such as bold or italic.) In addition to using the built-in styles, you can create your own customized styles.

To apply a built-in style:

1 Choose Format, Styles and Formatting to display the Styles and Formatting task pane.
2 Select the text to be formatted.
3 From the Pick formatting to apply list, select the desired style.

To create and apply a new character style:

1 Choose Format, Styles and Formatting to display the Styles and Formatting task pane.
2 Click New Style to open the New Style dialog box.
3 Under Properties, in the Name box, enter the name for the style.
4 From the Style type list, select Character.
5 Under Formatting, select the desired formats for the style.
6 Click OK to close the New Style dialog box.
7 Select the text to be formatted.
8 From the Pick formatting to apply list, select the new style you created.

Do it!

A-9: Applying character styles

Here's how	Here's why
1 Choose **Format, Styles and Formatting...**	To open the Styles and Formatting task pane. The Pick formatting to apply list displays all available formatting styles in the document.
2 Move to page 5	
Select **Project Justification**	Formatting of selected text **Arial, 14 pt, Bold** The formatting of the text appears in the Formatting of selected text box.
3 In the Pick formatting to apply list, click as shown	**Arial, 14 pt, Bol** **Arial, 14 pt, Bo** Normal + Font: Arial, 14 pt, Bold, Underline To apply the indicated style to the selected text.

4 Deselect the heading	The formatting of the heading now appears similar to the other headings in the document.
5 Click **New Style**	(The New Style button is in the Styles and Formatting task pane.) To open the New Style dialog box and create a new character style.
Edit the Name box to read **My style**	This will be the name of the style.
From the Style type list, select **Character**	
6 Under Formatting, select the options as shown	

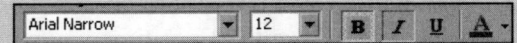

| Arial Narrow ▼ | 12 ▼ | **B** | *I* | U | A ▾ |

The new style will be Arial Narrow, 12 pt, bold, and italic.

Click **OK**	To close the New Style dialog box. The new style appears in the Pick formatting to apply list.
7 Move to page 2	
Select all the text under "Table of Contents"	Executive Summary, The Project Team, Project Justification, Progress Update, and Outstanding Issues for Phase One.
8 From the Pick formatting to apply list, select **My style**	
9 Deselect the text	The multiple formats included in the style are applied to the text in one step.
10 Close the Styles and Formatting task pane	
Update the document	

Topic B: Using tabs

This topic covers the following Microsoft Office Specialist exam objective.

#	Objective
WW03S-3-2	Setting, removing, and modifying tab stops

Tab stop types

Explanation

You can use tabs to align text in a document. *Tab stops* are predefined locations on the ruler. Each time you press the Tab key, the text is automatically moved to the first tab stop on the ruler. Tabs can be helpful for aligning columns of text.

Five types of tab stops are available. Each one has a different effect on text when you press the Tab key. The five tab options are described in the following table:

Tab	Description
Left-aligned	Text flows to the right of the tab stop.
Centered	Text is centered under the tab stop.
Right-aligned	Text flows to the left of the tab stop.
Decimal-aligned	Text aligns on the decimal point in numbers.
Bar	A vertical line is inserted under the tab stop.

Do it!

B-1: Examining tab stops

Here's how	Here's why
1 Open Tabs	(From the current unit folder.) Five types of tabs are set in this document.
2 Click within **Left-aligned text**	In the first paragraph.
3 Observe the ruler at the 3" mark	⌐ 1 ⌐ This is the Left Tab indicator. The text flows to the right of the tab stop.
4 Click within **Centered text**	The second block of text.
Observe the ruler at the 3" mark	⌐ 1 ⌐ This is the Center Tab indicator. The text is centered under the tab stop.
5 Click within **Right-aligned text**	
Observe the ruler	⌐ 1 ⌐ This is the Right Tab indicator. Text flows to the left of the tab stop.
6 Click within **1.23**	⌐ 1 ⌐ This is the Decimal Tab indicator. The numbers are aligned on the decimal point.
7 Click within **Bar tab**	⌐ 1 ⌐ This is the Bar Tab indicator. A vertical line divides the text at the 3" mark.
8 Close the document without saving	

Setting custom tabs

Explanation

By default, tab stops are set every 0.5" on the ruler. You can, however, set your own tab stops; this process clears the default tab stops. Setting your own tabs helps when you're creating headings for a memo or lining up text in a table. You can set tabs by using the Tab Alignment buttons, which are on the far left side of the ruler. These buttons look similar to the tab stop symbols on the ruler. By default, the Tab Alignment button sets a left-aligned tab. To choose one of the other tab types, click the button until you see the tab type you want.

To set a custom tab stop on the ruler:

1 Display the ruler, if necessary.

2 Select the paragraphs for which you want to set tabs.

3 Click the Tab Alignment button to select the type of tab you want to use.

4 Click the position on the ruler where you want to place the tab stop.

Moving custom tabs

You can move custom tab stops by dragging them to a new location on the ruler. Because the tabbed text is moved along with the tab stop, you can immediately see how the new tab stop will affect the text. To move a custom tab stop:

1 Select the paragraphs for which you want to move the custom tabs.

2 Drag the tab indicator to the new position on the ruler.

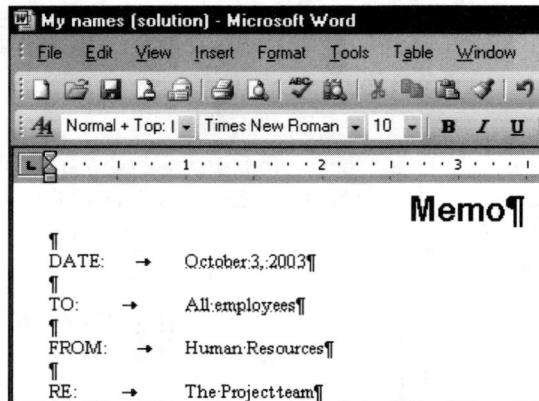

Exhibit 4-4: The left-aligned tab stop set at 1" in the document

Do it!

B-2: Setting and moving a custom tab stop

Here's how	Here's why
1 Open Names Save the document as **My names**	
2 Click after **DATE:**	To move the insertion point to the end of the line.
3 Press (TAB) twice	The default tab stops are set every 0.5".

4 Press ⌫BACKSPACE	To delete one of the tabs.
5 Insert the current date	(Choose Insert, Date and Time.) To add the current date to the document.
6 Click after **TO:**	
Press TAB	
Type **All employees**	To address this memo to everyone.
7 Place the insertion point after **FROM:**	
Press TAB	
Type **Human Resources**	To identify the sender.
8 Place the insertion point after **RE:**	
Press TAB	
Type **The project team**	
9 Select the paragraphs as shown	DATE:→4/14/2003¶ TO: → All·employees¶ FROM:→Human·Resources¶ RE: → The·project·team¶
Point as shown	L Left Tab
	(But do not click.) The Tab Alignment button on the ruler is set for a left tab.
10 Click at 2" on the ruler	To set a left-aligned tab stop at 2". The text flows to the right of the tab stop at 2".
11 Drag the tab stop to 1"	
Deselect the text and observe the screen	The text moves to the new tab stop position, as shown in Exhibit 4-4.
Update the document	

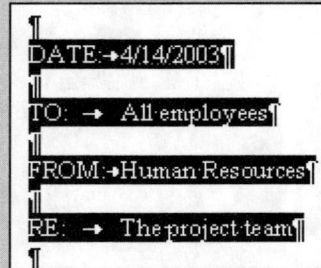

Clearing custom tabs

You can clear any or all custom tab stops. To do so, select the paragraph to be affected, and drag the tab indicator off the ruler and into the text area. When all custom tab stops are cleared, the default tab stops are automatically reset every 0.5" on the ruler.

To change the tab type, click the tab indicator. It will toggle through the following tab types: Left, Center, Right, Decimal, and Bar. There are additional settings, but you don't need to be concerned with them at this time.

Do it!

B-3: Clearing and setting other types of tabs

Here's how	Here's why
1 Select the DATE, TO, FROM, and RE paragraphs	
2 Point to the custom tab stop at 1"	The tab stop you set.
Drag the tab stop down off the ruler	To delete the custom tab stop you set. Word reverts to the default tabs every 0.5"
3 Click [L]	(The Tab Alignment button on the ruler.) When you click the button, it changes to a Center tab button: [⊥]
4 Click at 2" on the ruler	To set a center tab stop at 2". The text is centered under the tab stop.
Clear the center tab stop	Drag it off the ruler.
5 Click [⊥]	The Tab Alignment button changes to a Right tab button: [⌐]
6 Set a right-aligned tab stop at 2"	Click at 2" on the ruler.
7 Update and close the document	

Using the Tabs dialog box

Explanation

By using the Tabs dialog box, you can specify exact positions on the ruler that are difficult to set with the mouse. For example, if you want to set a tab stop at 4.18", you can type 4.18 in the Tab stop position box in the Tabs dialog box. The disadvantage of this technique is that you have to exit the dialog box to see the effect of the tab stop.

You can also use the Tabs dialog box to add a leader to a tab. A *leader* is a series of characters (such as dots or dashes) that fill in the spaces between tabbed text. Dot leaders are commonly used in tables of contents.

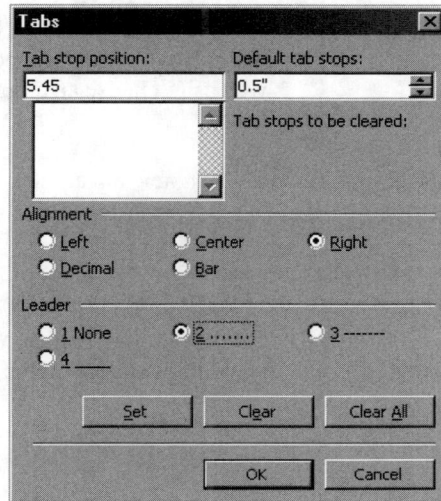

Exhibit 4-5: The Tabs dialog box

B-4: Setting a tab and leader in the Tabs dialog box

Here's how	Here's why
1 Verify that My project is open	
Move to page 2	If necessary.
2 Select all the paragraphs under Table of Contents	Executive Summary, The Project Team, Project Justification, Progress Update, and Outstanding Issues for Phase One.
3 Choose **Format**, **Tabs...**	To open the Tabs dialog box. You can use this dialog box to specify a position for tab stops, as well as to choose an alignment option and a leader.
4 In the Tab stop position box, enter **5.45**	To set a new tab at the 5.45" mark.
Under Alignment, select **Right**	
Under Leader, select **2**	To choose a dot leader. Your Tabs dialog box should now match Exhibit 4-5.
Click **OK**	
5 Deselect the text	You've set a right-aligned tab stop at 5.45" and added a dot leader.
6 Update the document	

Topic C: Paragraph formatting

This topic covers the following Microsoft Office Specialist exam objectives.

#	Objective
WW03S-2-2	Customizing and applying bullets and numbering
WW03S-3-2	Applying borders and shading to paragraphs
WW03S-3-2	Indenting, spacing and aligning paragraphs (This objective is also covered in Topic D.)

Paragraph formats

Explanation

There are several types of formatting you can apply to paragraphs. One common format is alignment. Paragraphs are aligned to the margins of a document or to the paragraph's left and right indents, if there are any. A *margin* defines the space at the upper, lower, left, and right sides of a document. You can also add bullets and numbers to paragraphs to create bulleted and numbered lists.

Selecting paragraphs

Before aligning paragraphs or applying any other paragraph formatting options, you must select the paragraphs you want to affect. However, unlike with character formatting, you don't need to select the entire paragraph to apply formatting to it. Instead, to select a single paragraph, click anywhere inside it. To select multiple paragraphs, select a part of each paragraph.

Repeating paragraph formatting

If you've just applied paragraph formatting and you want to apply it to another paragraph, you can press the F4 key, the shortcut for the Repeat command. You can also use the Format Painter to copy formatting to other paragraphs.

Paragraph alignments

The four alignment options for paragraphs are Left, Centered, Right, and Justified. You can apply these alignments by using the alignment buttons on the Formatting toolbar. The following table describes the alignment options and buttons:

Alignment	Button	Description
Left		Text is lined up evenly along the left side of the paragraph. The right side is *ragged*, which means that it's uneven.
Centered		Text is centered on the page or within the paragraph's indents. Both the left and right sides are ragged.
Right		Text is lined up evenly on the right side, and the left side is ragged. (Right-alignment is also called *flush-right*.)
Justified		Text is lined up evenly on both the left and right sides. Word adjusts the space between letters and words so that each line (except the last line) is even from side to side.

Do it!

C-1:   Using paragraph alignments

Here's how	Here's why
1 Move to page 1	
Place the insertion point anywhere in the title	You don't need to select the entire paragraph to apply paragraph formatting to it.
2 Observe the Alignment buttons on the Formatting toolbar	The Align Left button is selected.
Click	(The Align Right button.) The heading is right aligned.
Click	(The Justify button) The spacing between words is adjusted so that the heading lines up evenly between the two margins.
Click	(The Center button.) The heading is centered on page 1.
3 On page 3, click anywhere in the paragraph under "Executive Summary"	
Press (F4)	To repeat the formatting. The paragraph at the beginning of page 3 is centered.
4 Align the paragraph to the left	
5 Update the document	

Borders and shading

Explanation

You can add borders around text or paragraphs to set them apart from the remaining text. For example, a heading is an important part of a document report. You can add interest or emphasis to this heading by adding a border around it and shading it with a suitable color.

To add borders and shading:

1   Select the paragraph or text.
2   Choose Format, Borders and Shading to open the Borders and Shading dialog box.
3   Specify the border setting, style, and width by using the Borders tab.
4   Select a shading color from the Shading tab.
5   Click OK to close the dialog box.

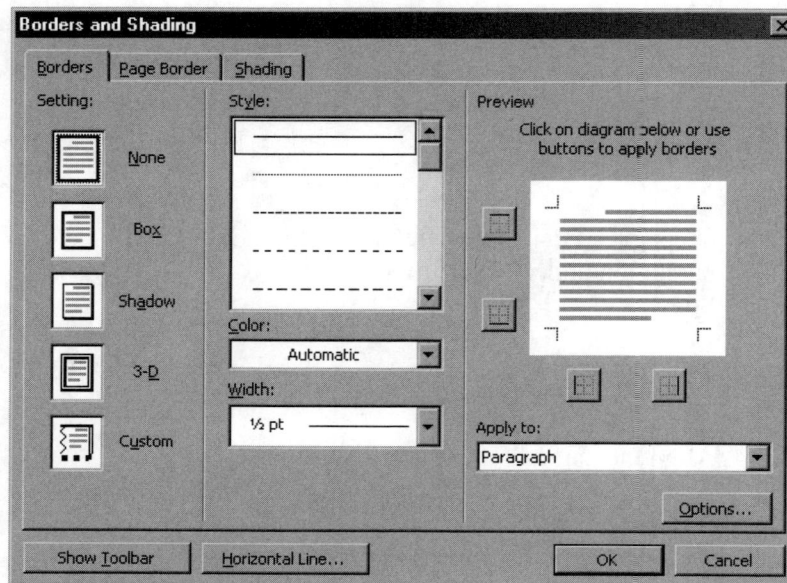

Exhibit 4-6: The Borders and Shading dialog box

Do it!

C-2: Applying borders and shading

Here's how	Here's why
1 Move to page 1	
Select the heading	
2 Choose **Format**, **Borders and Shading...**	To open the Borders and Shading dialog box, as shown in Exhibit 4-6.
3 Verify that the Borders tab is active	
Under Setting, select **Box**	The Preview area shows that a border has been applied to all four sides. You can use this area to modify some or all of the borders.
Observe the Style list	You can select different border styles for the heading by using this list.
Observe the Width list	By default, ½ pt is selected. You can change the width of the border by selecting different values from this list.
4 Under Preview, in the Apply to list, verify that Paragraph is selected	You'll apply the border to the selected heading.
5 Click the **Shading** tab	
Under Fill, select as shown	To shade the heading with the Gray-35% color.
Click **OK**	To close the Borders and Shading dialog box.
6 Deselect the heading	Outlander·Spices·™·Growth· Project·Progress·Report·for·Phase· One¶
	The heading has a border around it and is shaded with the color you selected.
7 Update the document	

Using bulleted and numbered lists

Explanation

When you're creating reports and other business documents, you might want to group information so that important sections stand out for the readers. You can organize and draw attention to lists by adding bullets and numbers.

To quickly add bullets or numbering to a list:

1 Select the paragraph you want to affect.

2 Click the Numbering button or the Bullets button on the Formatting toolbar.

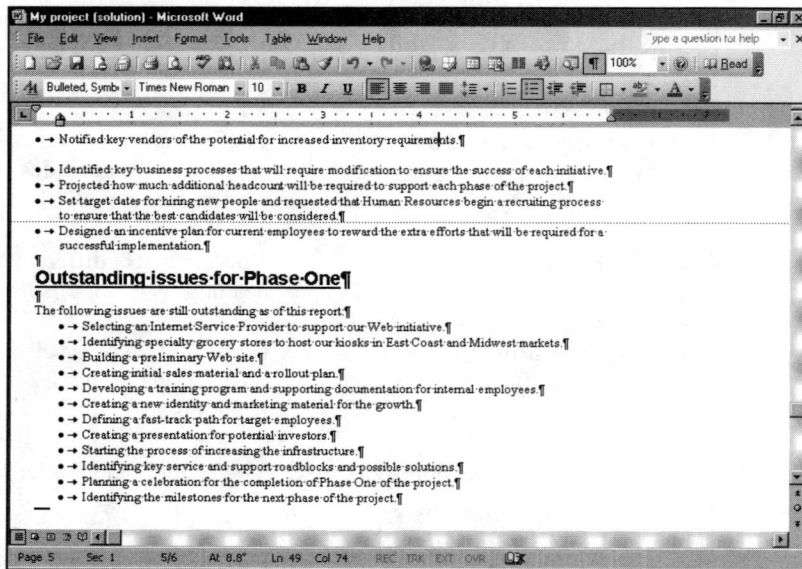

Exhibit 4-7: The bulleted list after Step 3 of the activity

Do it! **C-3: Adding bulleted and numbered lists**

Here's how	Here's why
1 Move to page 5	
Scroll down to see the bulleted list	Under Progress Update.
2 Move to the beginning of page 6	The Outstanding issues section.
Select all the paragraphs below the line "The following issues are still outstanding as of this report:"	
3 Click [≔]	(The Bullets button is on the Formatting toolbar.) To apply bullets to each paragraph in the selected text, as shown in Exhibit 4-7.
4 Move to the beginning of page 5	
Select as shown	

> Outlander·Spices·understands·that·the·wholesale·
> those·who·can·do·the·following·four·things:¶
> Keep·inventory·costs·and·levels·under·control.¶
> Provide·high-quality·products.¶
> Price·products·competitively.¶
> Control·cash·flow.¶

| 5 Click [≣] | (The Numbering button is on the Formatting toolbar.) To sequentially number the four items in the list. |
| 6 Update the document | |

Modifying bulleted and numbered lists

Explanation

You can also use the Bullets and Numbering dialog box to apply and modify the bullet and numbering styles. To open this dialog box, choose Format, Bullets and Numbering.

If you want to use pictures as bullets, you can create a custom style. You can also use the Picture Bullet dialog box to choose from a variety of picture bullets.

To use picture bullets:

1 Select the bulleted list to be affected.
2 Choose Format, Bullets and Numbering.
3 Click the Bulleted tab.
4 Click Customize to open the Customize Bulleted List.
5 Click Picture to open the Picture Bullet dialog box.
6 Select the specified picture.
7 Click OK to close the dialog box.

You can also change the format of the bullets and numbers in a list without affecting the text in the list. For example, you can change the color of bullets in a list without changing the text color. All you need to do is select one bullet or number, and all the bullets or numbers in the list are selected. Apply the different formatting options from the Formatting toolbar.

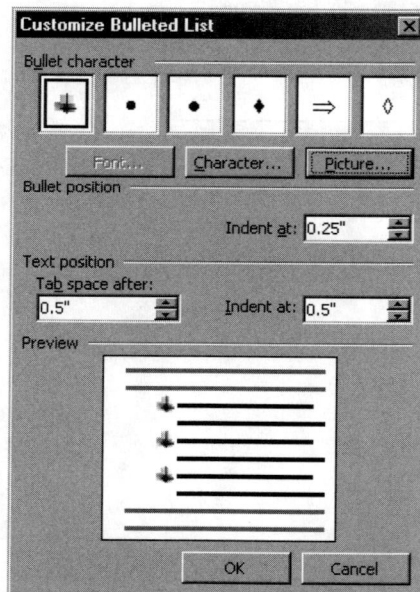

Exhibit 4-8: The Customize Bulleted List dialog box

Do it!   ## C-4:   **Editing bulleted and numbered lists**

Here's how	Here's why
1 Move to page 6	
Select the bulleted list	The list of outstanding issues.
2 Right-click and choose **Bullets and Numbering...**	(Within the selected text.) To open the Bullets and Numbering dialog box. This is where you select a different bullet type
3 Click **Customize**	To open the Customize Bulleted List dialog box.
4 Click **Picture**	To open the Picture Bullet dialog box. A list of bullets appears in the Picture Bullet dialog box.
Select a bullet of your choice	Scroll to view all available picture bullets.
Click **OK**	To close the Picture Bullet dialog box. The default bullet is replaced with the picture bullet, as shown in Exhibit 4-8.
5 Click **OK**	To close the Customize Bulleted List dialog box and see that the list has been formatted with the picture bullet you selected
6 Update the document and move to page 5	
Click the first bullet	
	To select only the bullets, not the text.
7 Display the Font Color list	Click the drop-down arrow next to the Font Color button on the Formatting toolbar.
Select Blue as shown	
Deselect the bullets	The bullets are blue; the text color is the same.
8 Update the document	

Using outline numbered lists

Explanation

There might be situations when you need to specify a sub-list for a numbered item list. You can use an outline numbered list to do this. For example, you might need to list the departments in your company and the employees in each department.

To insert an outline numbered list:

1 Select the text to be formatted.

2 Choose Format, Bullets and Numbering to open the Bullets and Numbering dialog box.

3 Click the Outline Numbered tab.

4 Select the numbering style.

5 Click OK.

Do it!

C-5: Adding an outline numbered list

Here's how	Here's why
1 Open Award	This document contains department names and employee names. You'll change this data to an outline numbered list.
Save the document as **My award**	
2 Place the insertion point as shown	¶ East·Coast¶ → Human·Resources·Department¶ → → Roger·Williams¶ → Accounting¶ → → Shannon·Lee¶
Select the text from **East Coast** through **Kevin Meyers**	
3 Choose **Format, Bullets and Numbering...**	To open the Bullets and Numbering dialog box.
Click the Outline Numbered tab	To view the various outline numbering styles. By default, None is selected.
4 Select the outline numbered style as shown	1) —— a) —— i) —— In the top row and second from the left.
Click **OK**	To close the dialog box.
Deselect the text	The text has changed to an outline numbered list.
5 Update and close the document	

Topic D: Advanced paragraph formatting

This topic covers the following Microsoft Office Specialist exam objectives.

#	Objective
WW03S-3-2	Indenting, spacing, and aligning paragraphs (This objective is also covered in Topic C.)
WW03E-1-2	Setting line and page breaks (This objective is also covered in the unit titled "Controlling page layout.")

Working with indents

Explanation

When working with long documents, you might want to set off certain blocks of text. You can do this by using indents. *Indents* define the left and right sides of a paragraph relative to the margins of the page. By default, indents are set to match the left and right margins. You can set indents without changing the margins of a document so that a block of text stands out from all the other text around it.

You can set indents through the Paragraph dialog box by choosing Format, Paragraph, or you can set indents by using the ruler. The ruler contains four indent markers. The following table describes these markers:

Indent marker	What it does
First-line indent	The down triangle on the left side of the ruler. Use it to control the left boundary for the first line of a paragraph.
Hanging indent	The up triangle on the left side of the ruler. Use it to control the left boundary of all lines in the paragraph *except* the first line.
Left indent	The box under the hanging-indent triangle. Use it to control the left indent for the entire paragraph.
Right indent	The up triangle on the right side of the ruler. Use it to control the right boundary of the paragraph.

To set indents, you drag the indent marker to a new location on the ruler. To set a new left or right indent for every line in a paragraph:

1 Click in the paragraph you want to indent, or, if there's more than one paragraph, select a part of each one.

2 On the ruler, drag the left indent or right indent marker to the indent position you want to apply.

First Line
indent marker

Hanging
indent marker

Right indent
marker

Left indent
marker

Executive·Summary¶

¶

Outlander·Spices·is·a·small,·privately·held·company·that·provides·exotic·spices·and·
gourmet·foods·to·restaurants·throughout·the·United·States.·We·have·twenty·kiosks·within·
gourmet·grocery·stores·on·the·West·Coast,·and·we·are·planning·to·launch·a·Web·initiative·
so·consumers·can·purchase·our·products·via·the·Internet.·We·also·plan·to·expand·our·
kiosk·operations·into·stores·on·the·East·Coast·and·in·the·Midwest·over·the·next·two·years.·
Because·this·is·an·aggressive·expansion·plan,·we·need·to·find·investment·capital·to·
ensure·our·success·going·forward.¶

¶

In·the·following·report,·you·will·find·an·overview·of·the·project·team·members,·a·
justification·for·the·project,·the·details·of·our·progress·on·this·initiative,·and·a·summary·
of·the·outstanding·issues·we·still·need·to·resolve.¶

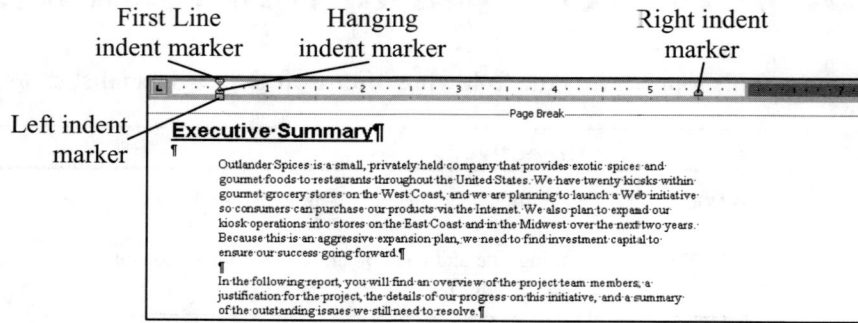

Exhibit 4-9: The indent markers on the ruler

Do it!   ## D-1:   Setting left and right indents

Here's how	Here's why
1 Move to page 4	In the document My project.
2 Click in the paragraph below "Thomas Boorman, IT Consultant"	The left and right indent markers are set at the margins of the document.
3 Drag the left indent marker to **0.5"**

The paragraph is indented. |
4 Click in the paragraph below "Solena Hernandez, Market Analyst"	
Set a left indent at **0.5"**	Drag the left indent marker on the ruler.
5 Click in the paragraph below "Susan Gianni, Business Consultant"	
Press F4	To repeat the indent formatting.
6 Repeat the formatting for all the team members	
7 Move to the beginning of page 3	You'll set indents for the Executive Summary section.
Select the paragraphs below "Executive Summary"	
Set a left indent at **0.5"**	
8 Drag the right indent marker to **5.5"**	
Deselect the text	You've indented both sides of the selected paragraphs, as shown in Exhibit 4-9.
9 Update the document	

Hanging indents

Explanation

Hanging indents affect all the lines in a paragraph except the first line. You use hanging indents for lists and to set off a paragraph. The paragraph you're now reading is an example of a hanging indent. The first line begins with the word "Explanation." All the lines below the first line are indented.

To set a hanging indent, you select the paragraph (or paragraphs) you want to affect, and then drag the hanging indent marker to another position on the ruler.

Do it!

D-2: Setting a hanging indent

Here's how	Here's why
1 Move to the beginning of page 5	
2 Click as shown	In·several·published·articles,·⌐ 1. → ▯ur·pricing·typically
Observe the ruler	The first-line, hanging indent, and left indent markers are flush with the left margin.
3 Select the three numbered paragraphs	You'll set a hanging indent for all three paragraphs at one time.
4 Drag the hanging indent marker to 0.5" as shown	
	The up triangle on the left side of the ruler.
5 Drag the first-line indent marker to 0.25" on the ruler	To align the numbers for all three paragraphs.
6 Update the document	

Creating a new line instead of a new paragraph

Explanation

Normally, you press Enter to start a new paragraph, and that new paragraph begins at the first-line indent marker. However, when working with paragraphs that contain hanging indents, you might want to start a new line at the hanging indent marker.

To create a new line that starts at the hanging indent, press Shift+Enter. This inserts a manual line break without creating a new paragraph.

Do it!

D-3: Comparing new lines and paragraphs

Here's how	Here's why
1 Place the insertion point at the end of the third paragraph	
Press ⏎ ENTER	You've created a new paragraph that begins at the first-line indent, not the hanging indent.
2 Press CTRL + Z	To undo the new paragraph.
3 Press SHIFT + ⏎ ENTER	·Inventory·typically·turns·over·*50%·faster* ness·and·shelf·life.·⏎
	To create a new line that starts at the hanging indent. The nonprinting character for the new line appears at the end of the paragraph, as shown above.
4 Press ← BACKSPACE	To delete the new line.
5 Update the document	

Working with paragraph and line spacing

Explanation

Another way to improve the readability and impact of your documents is to use line spacing and paragraph spacing. *Line spacing* controls the amount of vertical space between the lines of a paragraph. *Paragraph spacing* controls the amount of vertical space between paragraphs. You set both types of spacing by using the Paragraph dialog box.

Setting space before and after a paragraph

By default, there is no spacing between paragraphs. You might, however, want to increase the space above or below paragraphs to make text easier to read.

To change the amount of space before or after a paragraph:

1 Choose Format, Paragraph.
2 In the Paragraph dialog box, use the spinner controls to set the Before and After spacing. (You can also enter the spacing settings directly in the boxes.)
3 Click OK.

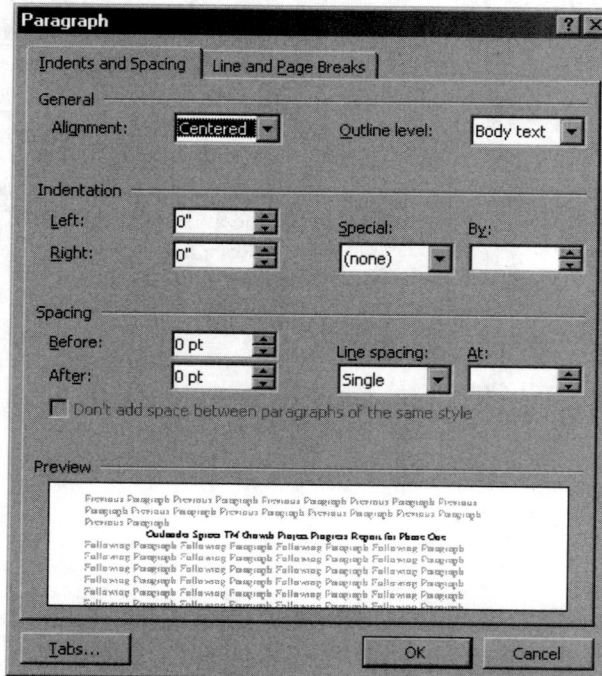

Exhibit 4-10: The Paragraph dialog box

Do it!

D-4: Setting the space before and after a paragraph

Here's how	Here's why
1 Move to the beginning of page 3	The Executive Summary heading and the paragraphs are located near the top of the page.
Verify that the insertion point is next to "Executive Summary"	
2 Choose **Format**, **Paragraph...**	To open the Paragraph dialog box, as shown in Exhibit 4-10. You can set paragraph alignments, indents, paragraph spacing, and line spacing in this dialog box.
Under Spacing, in the Before box, enter **90 pt**	Before: [90 pt]
Under Spacing, in the After box, enter **48 pt**	
Click **OK**	To close the Paragraph dialog box. You've increased the space above and below this paragraph on the page.
3 Update the document	

Line spacing

Explanation

Line spacing is set at single-spaced by default. Increasing the line spacing can sometimes improve readability and can be useful if you want to make a specific paragraph stand out or if you know that others will be editing the document and need room to write between the lines.

The following table lists the six options for line spacing:

Option	What it does
Single	Sets the line spacing to one line; this is the default.
1.5 lines	Sets the line spacing to one-and-a-half lines.
Double	Sets the line spacing to two lines.
At Least	Sets a minimum amount of space, which you specify, between lines.
Exactly	Sets an exact line spacing, which you specify, and does not adjust the spacing to accommodate changes in font size.
Multiple	Sets the line spacing to accommodate multiple lines. The default for this setting is three lines.

Do it!

D-5: Setting line spacing for a paragraph

Here's how	Here's why
1 Verify that the insertion point is on page 3	
Select the paragraphs below "Executive Summary"	
2 Click as shown	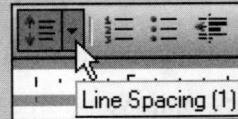
	The Line Spacing button is on the Formatting toolbar.
From the Line Spacing list, select as shown	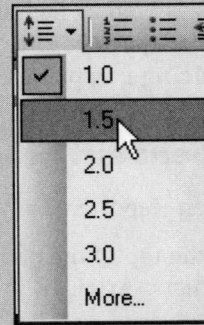
	To set the line spacing to 1.5 lines.
Deselect the text	You've increased the space between the lines.
3 Update and close the document	

Unit summary: Formatting characters and paragraphs

Topic A   In this topic, you learned how to apply **character formatting** to text in a document. You applied bold, italic, and underline formats. You also applied text effects. To apply formats, you used the Font dialog box, the repeat formatting feature, and the Format Painter. You also created a **character style** and applied it.

Topic B   In this topic, you learned about using **tabs** to align text. Using the ruler, you set tabs, moved tabs, and cleared tabs. You also used the Tabs dialog box to set a dot leader tab.

Topic C   In this topic, you learned about basic **paragraph formatting**. You applied borders and shading to paragraphs. You also aligned paragraphs and created numbered and bulleted lists. You also used outline numbered lists to create sub-lists for numbered lists.

Topic D   In this topic, you learned about advanced paragraph formatting. You set left and right **indents** as well as hanging indents. You also used **paragraph spacing** to control the amount of space before and after a paragraph. Finally, you learned how to change the **line spacing** in a paragraph.

Independent practice activity

1 Open Report and save it as **My Report**.

2 At the top of the page, select **Status Report** and apply the following character formats: Arial, 14 pt, Bold. Choose an underline style from the list. Select a text effect.

3 In the first paragraph under the heading, apply an italic format to **50%**.

4 For the lines **TO:**, **FROM:**, and **RE:**, set a left-aligned tab stop at 1".

5 Justify the first paragraph under the double line, and set the line spacing to 1.5.

6 Apply the bold format to the heading **The consultant team**.

7 Repeat the formatting for the headings **What's done** and **Still left to do**.

8 Use the Reveal Formatting task pane to compare the formatting of the text **Solena Hernandez, Market Analyst** with the formatting of the other team members' names. Apply the formatting of the rest of the names to the text **Solena Hernandez, Market Analyst**.

9 Apply bullets to the items under the headings "What's done" and "Still left to do."

10 For the paragraph under "Kathy Sinclair," set a left indent at 0.5" and a right indent at 4.5".

11 Repeat the indents for the paragraphs under "Thomas Boorman," "Solena Hernandez," and "Susan Gianni."

12 Center the heading **Status Report** at the top of the page.

13 Close the Reveal Formatting task pane.

14 Update the document and close it.

Review questions

1 What are the two ways to apply character formats?

2 Which key combination can be used to remove character formatting and return text to its underlying style?

   A `CTRL` + `SPACEBAR`

   B `CTRL` + `X`

   C `ALT` + `CTRL` + `SPACEBAR`

   D `ALT` + `DELETE`

3 Which formatting options can be used to display mathematical equations?

4 What technique should you use to apply the same highlighting multiple times?

5 Which of the following is a text effect.

   A Bold

   B Strikethrough

   C Marching Red Ants

   D Superscript

6 Which task pane is used to view the applied formatting to selected text?

7 Name the five types of tabs.

8 How do you change the tab type?

9 Which paragraph alignment avoids ragged edges?

10 Which command is used to change paragraph or line spacing?

11 How do you apply a border around a paragraph?

12 In what situation would you choose to create a numbered list instead of a bulleted list?

13 How do you change the format of the bullets without changing the bullet list text?

14 When working with paragraph indent markers, which of the following describes the left indent marker?

   A The up triangle at the right side of the ruler.

   B The box under the hanging indent triangle.

   C The up triangle on the left side of the ruler.

   D The down triangle on the left side of the ruler.

Unit 5

Creating and managing tables

Unit time: 40 minutes

Complete this unit, and you'll know how to:

A Create tables.

B Navigate, select elements, add text, and apply formatting in a table.

C Edit the structure of tables.

Topic A: Creating tables

This topic covers the following Microsoft Office Specialist exam objectives.

#	Objective
WW03S-2-1	Inserting new tables
WW03S-2-1	Converting text to tables

Creating a table

Explanation

A *table* is made up of rows and columns and is an excellent way to present information in a column layout. Although you can use tabs to manipulate text so that it appears to be in a table, this process can be time consuming. Tables are easier to use when you have a lot of text to align in each row or column. You can insert a table by choosing Table, Insert, Table or by using the Insert Table button.

When creating a table, you specify the number of rows and columns. The intersection of a row and a column is called a *cell*.

By default, Word places a border around a new table. If you remove the border, you'll see the table's gridlines. *Gridlines* provide a visual reference for the table's rows and columns. The gridlines are not visible when you print a document. You can hide or show gridlines by using the Table menu.

Using the Insert Table dialog box

Choose Table, Insert, Table to open the Insert Table dialog box. Here, you can specify the number of columns and rows the new table should have.

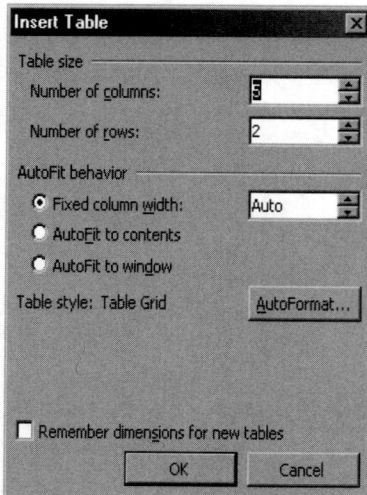

Exhibit 5-1: The Insert Table dialog box

Do it!

A-1: Creating a table by using the Insert Table dialog box

Here's how	Here's why
1 Open Update	From the current unit folder.
Save the document as **My update**	In the current unit folder.
Click ¶	(If necessary.) To show the nonprinting characters in the document.
2 Move to the end of the document	
3 Press (↵ ENTER) twice	To create two new blank lines.
4 Choose **Table**, **Insert**, **Table...**	To open the Insert Table dialog box, as shown in Exhibit 5-1.
5 Observe the Number of columns and Number of rows boxes	You can select the number of columns and rows by using the spin controls or by entering the numbers.
Set the Number of columns to **3**	
Set the Number of rows to **4**	
Click **OK**	To create a table with three columns and four rows. The insertion point is flashing inside the first cell.
6 Update the document	

Using the Insert Table button

Explanation

You can also insert a table by using the Insert Table button on the Standard toolbar. To do this:

1. Click where you want the table to appear.
2. Click the Insert Table button.
3. Drag to select the number of columns and rows you want to use.
4. Click the cell that will be the lower-right cell of the table.

Do it!

A-2: Creating a table by using the Insert Table button

Here's how	Here's why
1 Click in the last paragraph	Below the table you just inserted.
2 Press (↵ ENTER) twice	To create two blank rows.
3 Click ▦	(The Insert Table button is on the Standard toolbar.) To display the Insert Table button grid.
Drag as shown	3 x 4 Table To select a 3×4 table.
Click to insert the table	(Click the lower-right corner as shown above.) A table with three rows and four columns is inserted.
4 Update the document	

Creating tables from existing text

Explanation   You can convert existing text into a table; this will be faster than retyping or copying text into a new table. The text that you want to convert to a table needs to have separator characters to indicate where new columns should begin. A common separator character is a tab or comma. By default, paragraph marks indicate a new row. If the text doesn't contain separator characters, you can insert them before you proceed.

To convert text to a table:

1   Select the text to be converted into a table, including the paragraph marks. Make sure the text has separators, such as tab characters, where new columns should start.

2   Choose Table, Convert, Text to Table.

3   In the Convert Text to Table dialog box, Word suggests a number of columns and rows based on the separator characters.

4   Click OK.

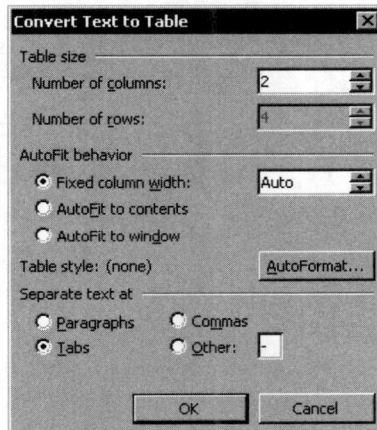

Exhibit 5-2: The Convert Text to Table dialog box

Do it!   **A-3:   Converting text to a table**

Here's how	Here's why
1 Select the four names of the project team members	¶ Thomas·Boorman → IT·Consultant¶ Elise·Sechan → Information·Technologies·Manager¶ Kathy·Sinclair → Project·Management·Consultant¶ Jack·Thomas → VP·Sales¶ ¶
2 Choose **Table**, **Convert**, **Text to Table...**	To open the Convert Text to Table dialog box, as shown in Exhibit 5-2. The selected text contains four paragraphs, so the table will have four rows. Also, tabs are specified as the separator characters, so the table will have two columns.
3 Click **OK**	To accept the default settings and convert the text to a table.
4 Deselect the text	Thomas·Boorman¤ | IT·Consultant¤ Elise·Sechan¤ | Information·Technologies·Manager¤ Kathy·Sinclair¤ | Project·Management·Consultant¤ Jack·Thomas¤ | VP·Sales¤ The project team members now appear in a two-column table.

Topic B: Working with tables

Explanation

You can move within a table by using the keyboard or the mouse. You can also select the various table elements and apply character formatting to the text in a table.

Moving within a table

To use the mouse to move in a table, click in a cell to place the insertion point in it. The following table lists the options for using the keyboard to move in a table:

Press this...	To do this...
(TAB)	Move one cell to the right.
(SHIFT) + (TAB)	Move one cell to the left.
(↑)	Move up one row.
(↓)	Move down one row.
(ALT) + (HOME)	Move to the first cell in the row.
(ALT) + (END)	Move to the last cell in the row.
(ALT) + (PAGE UP)	Move to the first cell in the column.
(ALT) + (PAGE DOWN)	Move to the last cell in the column.

B-1: Moving in a table

Here's how	Here's why
1 Verify that the insertion point is in the first cell of the third table	The four-column table.
2 Press (TAB)	To move one cell to the right.
Press (TAB)	To move one more cell to the right.
3 Press (SHIFT) + (TAB)	To move back one cell.
4 Press (↓) twice	To move down two rows.
5 Press (↑)	To move up one row.
6 Click the last cell of the table	
7 Move the insertion point back to the first cell	Use the keyboard or the mouse.

Selecting elements in a table

Explanation

There are situations when you'll need to select various parts of a table. For example, you might want to apply bold formatting to text in a cell or a row, or you might need to change the format of a cell border. To do this, you need to select the table element. When you select a table element, the element is highlighted. The following table lists the techniques for selecting table elements:

Element	Menu selection technique	Mouse selection technique
Cell	Place the insertion point in the cell, and choose Table, Select, Cell.	Point just inside the left side of the cell until the mouse pointer becomes a small, black arrow that points to the right. Then click.
Row	Place the insertion point anywhere in the row, and choose Table, Select, Row.	Point to the row in the selection bar, and then click.
Column	Place the insertion point anywhere in the column, and choose Table, Select, Column.	Point just inside the beginning of a column until the mouse pointer becomes a small, black arrow that points down. Then click.
Table	Place the insertion point in any cell, and choose Table, Select, Table.	Click the table-move handle that appears in the upper-left region of the table when the mouse pointer is over the table. You must be in Print Layout view to see the table-move handle.

Do it!   **B-2:   Selecting table elements**

Here's how	Here's why
1 Switch to Print Layout view	Choose View, Print Layout.
2 In the second table, click in the first cell	The three-column table.
3 Choose **Table**, **Select**, **Cell**	To select the first cell, where the insertion point is flashing.
4 In the selection bar, point to the first row of the table and click	To select the row.

5 Move the insertion point to any cell in the middle column	
Choose **Table**, **Select**, **Column**	To select the column.

6 Point to the table	⊞
	The table-move handle appears. You can use this handle to quickly select the entire table.
For the lower table, click ⊞	To select the entire four-column table.
7 Click any blank space in the document area	To deselect the table.

Adding text to a table

Explanation

After you've created a table, you're ready to add text or numbers to it. To do so:

1 Place the insertion point in the desired cell.

2 Type the text or numbers.

3 Press Tab to move one cell to the right. If you press Enter after typing, you'll create a new line in the same cell.

Do it!

B-3: Entering text in a table

Here's how	Here's why
1 In the last table, click in the first cell	
2 Type **Tasks**	
Press (TAB)	To move to the next cell.
3 Type **Who**	
Press (TAB)	
4 Type **Days** and move to the next cell	
5 Type **Comments**	In the last cell of the first row.
6 Press (TAB)	The insertion point moves to the first cell in the next row.
7 Complete the table as follows:	

Tasks	Who	Days	Comments
Find ISP	Boorman	4	In process
Identify milestones	Sinclair	1	

8 Update the document

Character and paragraph formatting in a table

Explanation

You might want to draw the reader's attention to a specific value in a cell. You can do this by adding character and paragraph formatting.

To apply character and paragraph formatting to the text in a table, you use the same techniques that you use to format text in a document.

Do it!

B-4: Formatting text in a table

Here's how	Here's why
1 Select the first row of the table	(In the selection bar, point to the row and click.) Because the first row contains headings, you'll format the headings to differentiate them from the other data.
2 Change the font to **Arial**	Use the Font list on the Formatting toolbar.
Click **B**	To apply bold to the text in the first row.
Deselect the text	The text in the first row is now Arial, bold.
3 Select the second column	
Click ≣	To center the text in the column.
4 Update the document	

Topic C: Modifying tables

This topic covers the following Microsoft Office Specialist exam objectives.

#	Objective
WW03S-2-1	Revising tables (insert and delete rows and columns, modify cell formats)
WW03E-2-3	Modifying table properties (This objective is also covered in *Word 2003: Intermediate*, in the unit titled "Formatting tables.")

Adding rows and columns

Explanation

As you work with a table, you might need to modify it by inserting a row or a column. When you insert a row, the height of the rows will not change. However, when you insert a column, the width of all the columns will be adjusted to keep the table within the page margins. You might also want to delete a row or column, change the width of a column, or even delete an entire table.

You can add rows and columns to a table by using the Table menu. You can also right-click the table and use the shortcut menu. The following table lists techniques for adding rows and columns:

To...	Do this...
Add a row to the end of a table	Place the insertion point in the last cell of the last row, and press Tab.
Add a row to the middle of a table	Select a row in the place where you want to insert the new row. Choose Table, Insert, Rows Above or Rows Below; or select the row, right-click, and choose Insert Rows.
Add multiple rows in the middle of a table	Select as many rows as you want to insert. Choose Table, Insert, Rows Above or Rows Below; or select the rows, right-click, and choose Insert Rows to insert the rows above the selected rows.
Add a column at the end of a table	Select all the end-of-row marks. Choose Table, Insert Columns, Columns to the Right; or select the end-of-row marks, right-click, and choose Insert Columns.
Add a column in the middle of a table	Select a column in the place where you want to insert a new column. Choose Table, Insert, Columns to the Left or Columns to the Right; or select a column, right-click, and choose Insert Columns to insert the column to the left of the selected column.
Add multiple columns in the middle of a table	Select as many columns as you want to add. Choose Table, Insert, Columns to the Left or Columns to the Right; or select multiple columns, right-click, and choose Insert Columns to insert columns to the left of the selected column.

Do it!

C-1: Adding rows and columns

Here's how	Here's why
1 In the last table, place the insertion point in the last cell	If necessary.
2 Press (TAB)	To add a new row at the bottom of the table.
3 In the new row, enter the Develop training task information as shown	

Tasks	Who	Days	Comments
Find ISP	Boorman	4	In process
Identify milestones	Sinclair	1	
Develop training	Thomas	25	Starts next week

4 Select the second row	Use the selection bar.
5 Choose **Table**, **Insert**, **Rows Above**	To add a new row above the selected row. Word inserts one row because you selected one row.
In the new row, enter the Build preliminary Web site task information as shown	

Tasks	Who	Days	Comments
Build preliminary Web site	Sechan	15	High priority
Find ISP	Boorman	4	In process
Identify milestones	Sinclair	1	
Develop training	Thomas	25	Starts next week

6 Select the second column	The Who column.
Right-click the selected column and choose **Insert Columns**	To insert one new column to the left of the selected column.
Click [↺ ▾]	(The Undo button is on the Standard toolbar.) To remove the newly inserted column.
7 Select the last three rows	
Right-click the selected rows and choose **Insert Rows**	To insert three rows above the selection.
8 Update the document	

Deleting columns, rows, and tables

Explanation

You can delete rows and columns from tables or delete an entire table by using commands in the Table menu. However, you can't delete rows, columns, or tables by using the Delete key. The Delete key deletes only the text in a table. The following table lists the techniques for deleting rows, columns, and an entire table:

To...	Do this...
Delete rows	Select the rows. Choose Table, Delete, Rows, or right-click and choose Table, Delete Rows.
Delete columns	Select the columns. Choose Table, Delete, Columns, or right-click and choose Table, Delete Columns.
Delete a table	Select the table. Choose Table, Delete, Table.

Tasks¤	Who¤	Days¤
Build·preliminary·Web·site¤	Sechan¤	15¤
Find·ISP¤	Boorman¤	4¤
Identify·milestones¤	Sinclair¤	1¤
Develop·training¤	Thomas¤	25¤

Exhibit 5-3: The table after Step 2 of the activity

Do it!

C-2: Deleting columns, rows, and an entire table

Here's how	Here's why
1 In the last table, select the three blank rows	If necessary.
Choose **Table**, **Delete**, **Rows**	To delete the rows. The remaining rows move up in the table.
2 Select the **Comments** column	In the lower table.
Right-click and choose **Delete Columns**	To delete the entire column, including its contents. Compare your screen to Exhibit 5-3.
3 Select the last table	Use the table-move handle.
Press (DELETE)	You've cleared the text from the table, but the table itself remains.
4 Click [↶ ▾]	To undo your deletion.
5 Place the insertion point within the second table	The empty table.
Choose **Table**, **Delete**, **Table**	To delete the entire table. Notice that you don't need to select the entire table in order to delete it.
6 Update the document	

Changing column width

Explanation

You can manually change the width of table columns by using the Table Properties dialog box or by dragging the column boundaries. You can also use the AutoFit feature to automatically change the width of the column to fit the text. When you change the width of one column, Word adjusts the width of the other columns to fit the table to the document margins. The following table lists the techniques for changing column width in a table:

When you use...	Do this...
The Table Properties dialog box	Select the column; choose Table, Table Properties; and use the spin controls to adjust the width.
The mouse	Point to the boundary of the column you want to change, and wait for the mouse pointer to become a double-headed arrow. Then, drag the boundary to the left or right to resize the column.
The AutoFit feature	Select the column, and choose Table, AutoFit, AutoFit to Contents.

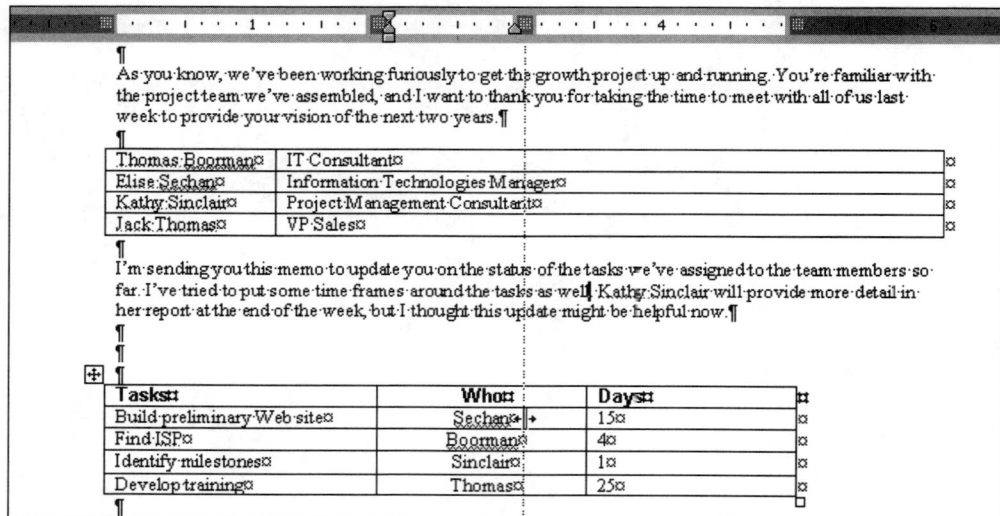

Exhibit 5-4: The column boundary being dragged in Step 6 of the activity

Do it! ## C-3: Changing the width of a column

Here's how	Here's why
1 Observe the first cell in the Tasks column	The cell contents wrap to a second line. You'll increase the width of the first column because there is enough space on the page.
2 Select the first column in the table	
3 Choose **Table, Table Properties...**	To open the Table Properties dialog box. By default, the Table tab is active.
Click the **Column** tab	
Increase the Preferred width to **2**	
Click **OK**	The width of the first column has increased, and all the text now fits on one line. The other column widths have decreased to keep the table within the margins.
Deselect the first column	
4 Point as shown	To the border between the Who and Days columns.

Tasks¤	Who¤	Days¤
Build·preliminary·Web·site¤	Sechan¤ ←‖→15¤	
Find·ISP¤	Boorman¤	4¤
Identify·milestones¤	Sinclair¤	1¤
Develop·training¤	Thomas¤	25¤

5 Press and hold the mouse, and observe the ruler	The box on the ruler represents the column boundary.
6 Drag to the left until the box on the ruler is over **3**	(As shown in Exhibit 5-4.) The width of the Who column has decreased.
7 Place the insertion point inside the table	If necessary.
8 Choose **Table, AutoFit, AutoFit to Contents**	

Tasks¤	Who¤	Days¤
Build·preliminary·Web·site¤	Sechan¤	15¤
Find·ISP¤	Boorman¤	4¤
Identify·milestones¤	Sinclair¤	1¤
Develop·training¤	Thomas¤	25¤

	To automatically resize the width of each column to fit its contents.
Click ¶	To hide the nonprinting characters in the document.
9 Update the document	

Aligning tables

Explanation   You can change a table's alignment by using the Table alignment options in the Table tab of the Table Properties dialog box. The alignment options include:

- **Left** — The table is aligned with the left margin.
- **Center** —The table is centered between the left and right margins.
- **Right** — The table is aligned with the right margin.

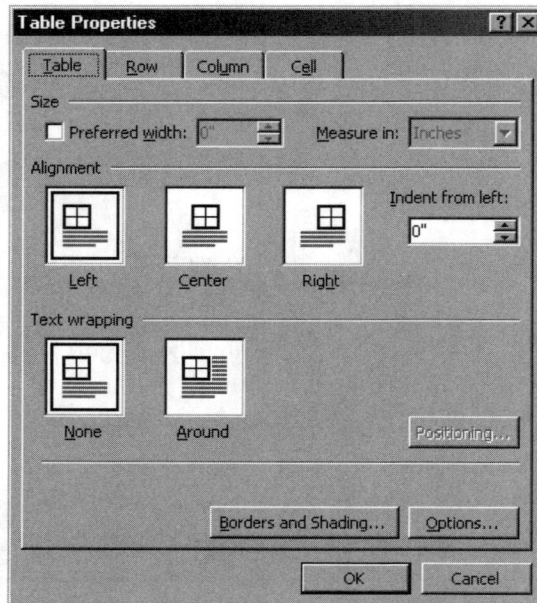

Exhibit 5-5: The Table Properties dialog box with the Table tab active

Do it!

C-4:   Aligning a table

Here's how	Here's why
1 Place the insertion point inside the table	If necessary.
2 Right-click and choose **Table Properties...**	To open the Table Properties dialog box.
Click the **Table** tab	To view the options in the Table tab, as shown in Exhibit 5-5. The Alignment options (Left, Center, and Right) enable you to change the position of the table with respect to the margins.
Click **Center**	
Click **OK**	The table is centered between the left and right margins.
3 Update and close the document	

Unit summary: Creating and managing tables

Topic A   In this topic, you learned that **tables** provide a structured way to present information. You learned that to create tables, you could use the Insert Table command or the Insert Table button. You can also **convert text** to a table.

Topic B   In this topic, you learned how to **navigate in a table** by using the keyboard. You also learned that you could select any table element by using the commands in the **Table, Select** submenu. Then, you learned how to add text in a table and how to apply character and paragraph formatting to the text.

Topic C   In this topic, you learned how to modify tables by **adding rows** and **columns** and by deleting rows, columns, and tables. You also learned how to **change column widths**. Finally, you learned how to **align a table**.

Independent practice activity

1 Create a new, blank document.

2 Insert a table with four columns and four rows.

3 Add the text in the first four rows, as shown in Exhibit 5-6. You'll format the text later.

4 Add a fifth row to the table.

5 Add the text in the fifth row, as shown in Exhibit 5-6.

6 Select the first row.

7 Format the font as Arial, 14 pt, Bold.

8 Center the text in the first row.

9 Change the width of the last column to accommodate all text on one line. (*Hint:* Use AutoFit.)

10 Save the document as **Tea** in the current unit folder.

11 Compare your table to Exhibit 5-6.

12 Close the document.

Tea	Vendor	Order status	Comments
Oolong	East Seas	In route	2 weeks later
Darjeeling	China Clipper	In warehouse	Excellent
Early Grey	House of Lords	In warehouse	Not fresh-consider other options
House Blend	China Clipper	Shipping next week	New product for this vendor

Exhibit 5-6: The Tea document after Step 10 of the Independent Practice Activity

Review questions

1 Why is it better to create a table instead of using tabs to align text in a document?

2 What are the lines that indicate columns and rows in a table but do not appear when printed called?

   A Outlines

   B Guides

   C Borders

   D Gridlines

3 Name two ways to create a table in a document.

4 When you convert existing text into a table, how is the text divided into rows and columns?

5 What is the shortcut method for using the Table, Insert, Rows Above command?

6 How can you insert multiple columns in the middle of a table?

7 What happens when you use the Delete key in a table?

8 How do you delete a column from a table?

9 Which method enables you to specify row height with the best accuracy?

   A Using the Table Properties box

   B Dragging the row boundary with the mouse

   C Using the AutoFit feature

   D Using the Table, Row, Set Height command

10 What are the three ways to align a table?

Unit 6

Controlling page layout

Unit time: 40 minutes

Complete this unit, and you'll know how to:

A Add headers and footers to a document.

B Set and change the margins of a document.

C Add and delete manual page breaks.

Topic A: Creating headers and footers

This topic covers the following Microsoft Office Specialist exam objective.

#	Objective
WW03S-3-4	Inserting and modifying content in document headers and footers

Headers and footers

Explanation

A *header* is the text that prints at the top of the page. A *footer* is the text that prints at the bottom of the page. You can enter data into a header or a footer by using the Header and Footer toolbar.

To enter data into a header or a footer, you need to open the header and footer area in a document. Do this by double-clicking on the header and footer area or by choosing View, Header and Footer.

Headers and footers are not visible in Normal view. To see them on-screen, you need to switch to Print Layout view. Even if the header and footer text isn't visible, it will be included in the printed document.

To create a header or footer, choose View, Header and Footer. When you do this, you can see the header and footer because Word automatically switches to Print Layout view. This view also displays the page breaks and margins in a document. You can type your header and footer or use the Header and Footer toolbar to insert text.

The Header and Footer toolbar

The Header and Footer toolbar automates common header and footer options and tasks. For example, you can use it to insert the current date or page numbers. The most commonly used options are shown as buttons on the toolbar. The other options are listed under the Insert AutoText button. In addition to inserting common entries, you can also use the toolbar to move between the headers and footers.

Exhibit 6-1: The Header and Footer toolbar

The following table explains the various options on the Header and Footer toolbar:

Button	Name	Used to
	Insert Page Number	Insert page numbers that are automatically updated when you add or delete pages.
	Insert Number of Pages	Insert the total number of pages in the document.
	Format Page Number	Open the Page Number Format dialog box, where you can format the page number.
	Insert Date	Insert the current system date.
	Insert Time	Insert the current system time.
	Page Setup	Open the Page Setup dialog box, where you can specify margin, paper, and layout settings.
	Show/Hide Document Text	Show or hide text in a document when the header and footer area is active.
	Same as Previous	Apply the same header or footer or have different headers and footers. By default, the Same as Previous button will be disabled.
	Switch Between Header and Footer	Switch between the header and footer of a page.
	Show Previous	Shift the insertion point to the previous header or footer area.
	Show Next	Shift the insertion point to the next header or footer area.

Do it!   **A-1:   Exploring the header and footer areas**

Here's how	Here's why
1 Open Progress	From the current unit folder.
Save the document as **My progress**	
2 Display the nonprinting characters	If necessary.
3 Choose **View**, **Header and Footer**	The document view changes to Print Layout view, and the header and footer area opens. The dotted-line rectangle indicates the header area. The insertion point is in the left corner. The Header and Footer toolbar also appears, as shown in Exhibit 6-1.
Press (TAB)	The insertion point moves to the center of the header area.
Observe the ruler	This is a center tab stop.
4 Press (TAB) and observe the ruler	This is a right aligned tab stop.
5 Click 🖳	(The Switch Between Header and Footer button is on the Header and Footer toolbar.) To move to the footer. You use this button to switch between the header and footer.
Click 🖳 again	To move back to the header again.
6 Click **Close**	(The Close button is on the Header and Footer toolbar.) To close the toolbar and the header and footer area.
7 Update the document	

Adding text and AutoText entries to headers and footers

Explanation
You can use text of your choice as a page header. By default, the insertion point is at the left edge of the header and footer area.

To enter text, you begin typing. If you want to use an AutoText entry, click the Insert AutoText button and select the entry.

You can change the alignment by using the preset tab stops or by clicking the alignment buttons on the Formatting toolbar.

Do it!

A-2:   Adding information to headers and footers

Here's how	Here's why
1 Choose **View**, **Header and Footer**	To open the header and footer area.
2 Click 🗒	(The Insert Date button is on the Header and Footer toolbar.) To add the current date at the left side of the header.
3 Press → twice	To move to the right side of the header area.
Type your name	To add your name to the header. Your name is right aligned.
4 Click 🗐	To switch to the footer.
Press TAB	To move to the center of the footer area.
5 Click **Insert AutoText**	Insert AutoText ▾ # - PAGE - Author, Page #, Date Confidential, Page #, Date Created by Created on Filename Filename and path Last printed Last saved by Page X of Y (The Insert AutoText button is on the Header and Footer toolbar.) You'll see a list of the AutoText entries that you can insert in the header or footer.
6 Select **Page X of Y**	To insert an AutoText page number entry in which the X represents the current page and Y represents the total number of pages.
Click **Close**	
7 Update the document	

Editing text in headers and footers

Explanation

You can edit the text in a header or a footer by using the same editing techniques you use in the document area. You can also delete a header or a footer. To edit the text in a header or a footer:

1 Choose View, Header and Footer.
2 Select the text.
3 Modify the text as needed, or press Delete to remove it.

Do it!

A-3: Editing headers and footers

Here's how	Here's why
1 Open the header and footer area	Choose View, Header and Footer.
2 Select your name	In the header.
3 Press (DELETE)	To delete your name.
4 Type **Outlander Spices**	To add the company name to the header.
5 Switch to the footer	
6 Drag the mouse over all the text in the footer area	To select the entire footer.
7 Click **Insert AutoText**	
Select **Confidential, Page #, Date**	You've inserted the word "Confidential," the page number, and the date in the footer.
8 Delete the date in the header	Move to the header, select the date, and press Delete.
Press (DELETE)	To delete the tab and center "Outlander Spices" in the header.
9 Click **Close**	
Update the document	

Topic B: Working with margins

This topic covers the following Microsoft Office Specialist exam objectives.

#	Objective
WW03S-3-5	Modifying page margins, page orientation
WW03E-1-2	Controlling orphans and widows

Margins

Explanation

Margins define the amount of space between the text and the upper, lower, left, and right edges of the page. By default, the top and bottom margins are set at 1" and the left and right margins at 1.25". You can set custom margins for a document, but there are a couple of things to keep in mind. First, in general, margins affect all the pages of a document. Second, headers and footers are contained in the top and bottom margins. So make sure you don't decrease the margins too much, or the header and footer information might not print completely.

You can adjust the margins by using Print Layout view or by using the Margins tab of the Page Setup dialog box.

Adjusting margins in Print Layout view

You can adjust the margins in Print Layout view by dragging the margin boundaries. You can see the effect on the page immediately. Print Layout view displays horizontal and vertical rulers, which you can use as guides.

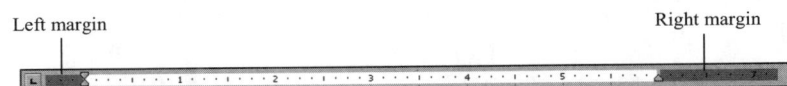

Exhibit 6-2: The left and right margins on the horizontal ruler

The left margin boundary on the horizontal ruler is between the left indent and first-line indent markers. The right margin boundary is above the right indent marker. To move any margin boundary, you need to drag it. When you point to the margin boundary, the mouse pointer becomes a double-headed arrow.

The top margin boundary is at the upper intersection of the gray and white areas of the vertical ruler. The bottom margin boundary is at the lower intersection of the gray and white areas.

To change the margins:

1. Choose View, Print Layout, or click the Print Layout View button.
2. To change the left and right margins, place the mouse pointer over the left or right margin boundary on the horizontal ruler. To change the top and bottom margins, place the mouse pointer over the top or bottom margin boundary on the vertical ruler.
3. Drag the margin boundary to a new location on the ruler, and release the mouse.

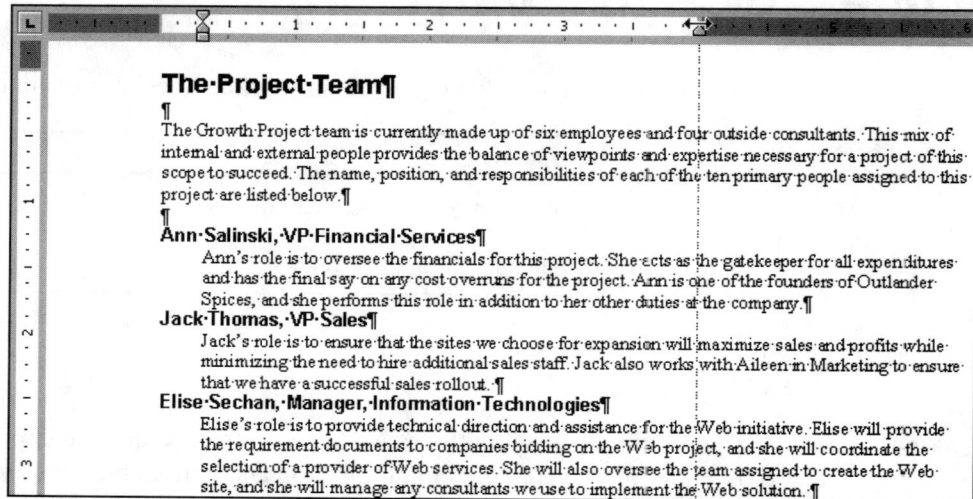

Exhibit 6-3: The right margin boundary adjusted by dragging in Step 5 of the activity

Do it!

B-1: Using Print Layout view to adjust margins

Here's how	Here's why
1 Move to page 4	The Project Team page.
2 Choose **View**, **Print Layout**	(If necessary.) To switch to Print Layout view. You can see indent markers on the horizontal ruler, as shown in Exhibit 6-2.
3 Point between the left indent and first-line indent markers
(On the ruler.) When you move the mouse pointer over the left margin boundary, the pointer changes to a double-headed arrow.
4 Point directly above the right indent marker	When you move the mouse pointer over the right margin boundary, the pointer changes to a double-headed arrow.
5 Drag the right margin to **4**	(On the ruler, as shown in Exhibit 6-3.) The right edge of the text shifts to the left, and there is additional white space on the right side of the page.
6 Point to the bottom margin boundary on the vertical ruler	At the lower intersection of the gray and white sections of the ruler.
7 Drag the bottom margin boundary up to **7"**, as shown
The lower edge of the text shifts up, and there is additional white space at the bottom of the page.
8 Scroll through the document	The right and bottom margins have been changed throughout the entire document.
9 Update the document	

The Page Setup dialog box

Explanation

You can also adjust margins by using the Margins tab of the Page Setup dialog box. To increase or decrease each margin, you can use the spin controls or enter the desired values. By using the Page Setup dialog box, you can specify an exact measurement for each margin. After you specify the margins, you must close the dialog box and preview the document to see the effect of the new margins.

To change margins by using the Page Setup dialog box:

1   Choose File, Page Setup.
2   Click the Margins tab.
3   Use the spin controls to adjust margins, or type a new measurement in the text box for each margin.
4   Click OK.

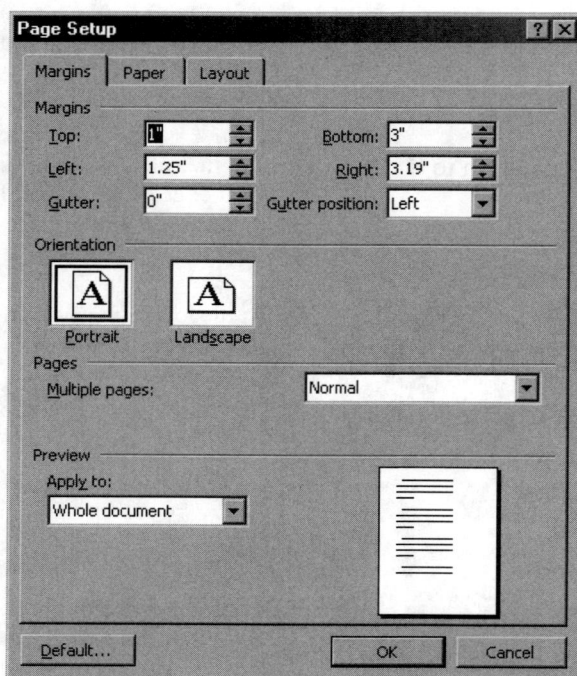

Exhibit 6-4: The Margins tab of the Page Setup dialog box

Do it!

B-2: Using the Page Setup dialog box to adjust margins

Here's how	Here's why
1 Choose **File**, **Page Setup...**	To open the Page Setup dialog box, as shown in Exhibit 6-4.
Observe the margin settings for the Bottom and Right margins	These are the margins you set by using Print Layout view.
Observe the margin settings for the Top and Left margins	These are still Word's default settings.
2 Use the spinner controls to change the Bottom margin to **1**	
3 Press (TAB) twice	To move to the Right text box.
Enter **1.25**	To set the right margin to 1.25".
Click **OK**	To apply the changes. You've reset the margins to Word's default values.
4 Update the document	

Page orientation and vertical alignment

Explanation

For certain documents, such as charts, tables, certificates, or mailers, you might choose to print in landscape orientation instead of the default portrait orientation. You can change the orientation for the entire document or only certain parts of the document.

As you work with different page layouts, you might also want to adjust the vertical alignment of your text. You can adjust text vertically to align with the top of the page, the center of the page, or the bottom of the page, or you can justify the text between the top and bottom margins.

To change the orientation of a document:

1 Choose File, Page Setup to open the Page Setup dialog box.

2 Click the Margins tab.

3 Under Orientation, click Landscape.

4 Activate the Layout tab. In the Apply to box, select Whole document to apply the new settings to the entire document. Or, to apply the new setting to the selected text only, select Selected text in the Apply to box.

5 Click OK.

To change the vertical alignment of a document:

1 Choose File, Page Setup to open the Page Setup dialog box.

2 Click the Layout tab.

3 Next to Vertical alignment, select the type of alignment you want to use.

4 Click OK.

Do it!

B-3: Setting page orientation and vertical alignment

Here's how	Here's why
1 Choose **File**, **Page Setup...**	(To open the Page Setup dialog box.) You'll change the orientation of this document.
Verify that the Margins tab is activated	To access the paper size and orientation options.
2 Under Orientation, click **Landscape**	To select landscape as the orientation for the document.
3 Under Preview, in the Apply to box, verify that Whole document is selected	To apply the orientation settings to the entire document.
4 Click the **Layout** tab	To access the vertical alignment options.
5 Under Page, from the Vertical alignment list, select **Center**	
	To center the text vertically.
Click **OK**	To close the Page Setup dialog box. The document text appears centered on the landscape page.
6 Update the document	

Text flow options

Explanation

As you adjust margins and page orientation of a document, you might cause headings to become separated from their corresponding paragraphs. You can fix this by selecting the headings and selecting Keep with next in the Line and Page Breaks tab of the Paragraph dialog box.

You might want to ensure that a paragraph doesn't get split between pages. For this, apply the Keep lines together option in the Line and Page Breaks tab of the Paragraph dialog box.

You can also control widow and orphan lines. A *widow* is a paragraph's last line printed by itself at the beginning of a page. An *orphan* is a paragraph's first line printed by itself at the bottom of a page. The option for controlling widows and orphans is in the Line and Page Breaks tab of the Paragraph dialog box. The option is selected by default.

To control the flow of text to keep lines or paragraphs together:

1 Select the text you want to keep together.

2 Choose Format, Paragraph to open the Paragraph dialog box.

3 Click the Line and Page Breaks tab.

4 Under Pagination, select the text flow option you want to apply.

5 Under Pagination, verify that the Widow/Orphan Control box is checked. If not, check it.

6 Click OK.

Do it!

B-4:   Applying text flow options

Here's how	Here's why
1 Move to page 4	If necessary.
Observe the paragraph below "Solena Hernandez"	(At the bottom of page 4.) The first line is separated from the next line. This is an orphan.
2 Select the first line of the paragraph below "Solena Hernandez"	You'll control the orphan in this paragraph.
3 Choose **Format, Paragraph...**	To open the Paragraph dialog box.
Click the **Line and Page Breaks** tab	
4 Under Pagination, check **Widow/Orphan control**	
Click **OK**	The entire paragraph is now together on the next page.
5 Select **Solena Hernandez, Market Analyst**	The automatic page break separates her name from the paragraph describing her. You'll apply text flow options to keep this heading on the same page as the paragraph.
6 Open the Paragraph dialog box	Choose Format, Paragraph.
Verify that the Line and Page Breaks tab is activated	
7 Under Pagination, check **Keep with next**	To keep the heading with the paragraph following it.
Click **OK**	
8 Update the document	

Topic C: Working with page breaks

This topic covers the following Microsoft Office Specialist exam objectives.

#	Objective
WW03S-3-5	Inserting and deleting page breaks (This objective is also covered in *Word 2003: Intermediate*, in the unit titled "Working with sections and columns.")
WW03E-1-2	Setting line and page breaks (This objective is also covered in the unit titled "Formatting characters and paragraphs.")

Page breaks

Explanation

When there is more text on a page than the margins can accommodate, a new page is created by inserting a separator called a *page break*. The process of separating text into pages is called *pagination*. Page breaks do not always occur where you want them to be, so when you've completed a long document, you'll need to paginate it manually by adding page breaks. Pagination is affected by the margins, the page orientation, and the size and amount of text (or graphics) on a page. *Page orientation* controls whether the text on the page is set to print as 8.5" x 11" (portrait) or 11" x 8.5" (landscape). Most business documents have a portrait orientation. Any time you change margins or the page orientation, you should check your pagination before printing the document.

Types of page breaks

You'll see two types of page breaks: automatic and manual. An *automatic page break* is one that Word inserts when the amount of text exceeds the vertical margins. Automatic page breaks appear as widely spaced dotted lines. A *manual page break* is one you insert. Manual page breaks appear as closely spaced dotted lines with the words "Page Break" inserted in the middle of the line.

Adding a manual page break

You can insert a manual page break by using the Insert, Break command or by pressing Ctrl+Enter. To insert a manual page break:

1   Place the insertion point directly to the left of the text that you want on the new page.
2   Press Ctrl+Enter, or choose Insert, Break, select Page break, and click OK.

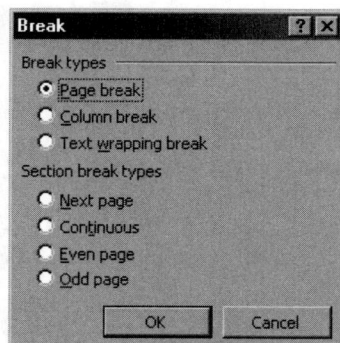

Exhibit 6-5: The Break dialog box

Do it!   **C-1: Adding manual page breaks**

Here's how	Here's why
1 Choose **View**, **Normal**	To switch to Normal view.
2 Move to the beginning of the document	Under the heading on the first page, you'll see a dotted line with the words "Page Break" in the center. This is a manual page break.
3 Click the page break	To select the manual page break.
4 Scroll down to see the "Progress Update" heading	(Near the beginning of page 6.) The dotted line in the middle of the bulleted list is an automatic page break.
Point to the automatic page break, and click	You can't select an automatic page break.
5 Place the insertion point as shown	¶ **Progress·Update¶** ¶
6 Choose **Insert**, **Break...**	To open the Break dialog box, as shown in Exhibit 6-5.
Verify that Page break is selected	
Click **OK**	To insert a manual page break.
7 Press (PAGE DOWN)	The automatic page break is removed.
8 Place the insertion point as shown	**Outstanding·Issues·for·Phase·One¶** ¶
Press (CTRL) + (↵ ENTER)	To insert a manual page break.
9 Update the document	

Deleting manual page breaks

Explanation

To delete a manual page break, select it and press Delete. You can't delete an automatic page break by using the Delete key because it was inserted automatically to accommodate the text. If you want to delete an automatic page break, place a manual page break above it. Then, the automatic page break will be removed automatically.

If you delete a manual page break, make sure you check your pagination before you print. This is to ensure that an automatic page break has not been added.

Do it!

C-2: Deleting a page break

Here's how	Here's why
1 Move to the beginning of the document	
2 Select the manual page break below the heading on page 1	Point to it and click.
3 Press (DELETE)	The manual page break is gone, and the heading is now on the same page as the Table of Contents.
4 Scroll to observe the screen	Word inserted an automatic page break above the last entry in the Table of Contents.
5 Reinsert a manual page break before "Table of Contents"	Press Ctrl+Z to undo the deletion. If you need to, you can press Ctrl+Enter to reinsert the manual page break.
6 Update and close the document	

Unit summary: Controlling page layout

Topic A
In this topic, you learned that **headers** and **footers** can be used to add information such as dates and page numbers to documents. You learned how to create headers and footers by adding text and by using **AutoText** entries. You also edited headers and footers and deleted them.

Topic B
In this topic, you learned how to control how close your text is to the edge of the page by setting **margins**. You set margins by dragging them in Print Layout view and then by using the **Page Setup dialog box**. You also kept text together by using text flow options, such as **Widow/Orphan control**.

Topic C
In this topic, you learned how to force text to begin on a new page by inserting **page breaks**. You identified and added manual page breaks. You also deleted manual and automatic page breaks.

Independent practice activity

1 Open Status and save it as **My status**.

2 Add the date to the center of the header.

3 Add **Outlander Spices** to the footer.

4 Adjust the left and right margins to 1.5" and the top margin to 1.5".

5 Insert a page break above the heading "Progress to date."

6 Update the document and close the file.

Review questions

1 What are the two ways to open the header and footer area?

2 How do you save a new header and footer?

3 Which button on the Header and Footer toolbar would you use to add the Filename in your header?

   A Page Setup

   B Insert AutoText

   C Filename

   D Insert Properties

4 What are the top, bottom, left, and right default margin settings?

5 Which view enables you to adjust the page margins by dragging the margin boundaries?

6 How do you access the Page Setup dialog box?

7 What are the steps for changing the page orientation?

8 Which dialog box is used to control widows and orphans?

A Page Setup

B Paragraph

C Print Layout

D Page Break

9 True or False. You can delete an automatic page break?

Unit 7

Proofing and printing documents

Unit time: 30 minutes

Complete this unit, and you'll know how to:

A Proof a document and use the Thesaurus.

B Preview and print documents.

Topic A: Checking spelling and grammar

This topic covers the following Microsoft Office Specialist exam objectives.

#	Objective
WW03S-1-1	Checking spelling and grammar
WW03S-1-1	Checking language usage (e.g., Thesaurus)
WW03S-1-6	Using the Research tool to select and insert supporting text-based information
WW03E-5-3	Setting default dictionary

Checking a document's spelling automatically

Explanation

When you've finished writing a document, it's a good idea to proof it by checking its spelling and grammar. Misspelled words and poor grammar can distract readers from the content of the document. The Spelling and Grammar feature can help you proof your document. This feature can be used in automatic mode to correct words as you work, or you can wait until you've completed the document and then check its spelling and grammar. While writing or proofing a document, you might decide that certain words can be replaced by more suitable words with similar meanings. To do this, use the Thesaurus feature.

By default, the Spelling and Grammar feature is set to automatic mode. In this mode, Word checks the spelling of words against its dictionary as you type. Misspelled words in the document are underlined with a wavy red line. To correct these words:

1 Select the word that is underlined in red.

2 Right-click to display the shortcut menu, and then choose one of the following:

- The correct spelling (if it's listed)

- Ignore All, if you want to leave the word spelled the way it is

- Add to Dictionary, if you want to add the word to Word's dictionary

Do it!

A-1: Using the automatic spelling checker

Here's how	Here's why
1 Open Spelling	From the current unit folder.
Save the document as **My spelling**	
2 Move to page 3	The Executive Summary page.
3 Observe the word **individul**	The wavy red underline indicates a spelling error.
4 Right-click **individul**	To open the shortcut menu.
Choose **individual**	

> individual
>
> Ignore All
> Add to Dictionary
> AutoCorrect   ▶
> Language   ▶
> ABC Spelling...
> Look Up...
> ✂ Cut
> Copy
> Paste

To enter the correct spelling.

5 Update the document

Checking a document's spelling manually

Explanation

The Spelling and Grammar feature can be run manually to check the spelling in an entire document at one time. Using the Spelling and Grammar dialog box, you can correct spelling, ignore spelling, and add words to the dictionary.

To check the spelling of a document manually:

1 Move to the beginning of the document.

2 Choose Tools, Spelling and Grammar.

3 Choose any option in the Spelling and Grammar: English (U.S.) dialog box:

- If the correct word is in the Suggestions box, select it and click Change. You can click Change All to change all occurrences of the word.

- Click Ignore Once or Ignore All to leave the word spelled the way it is.

- Click Add to Dictionary to add the word to the dictionary.

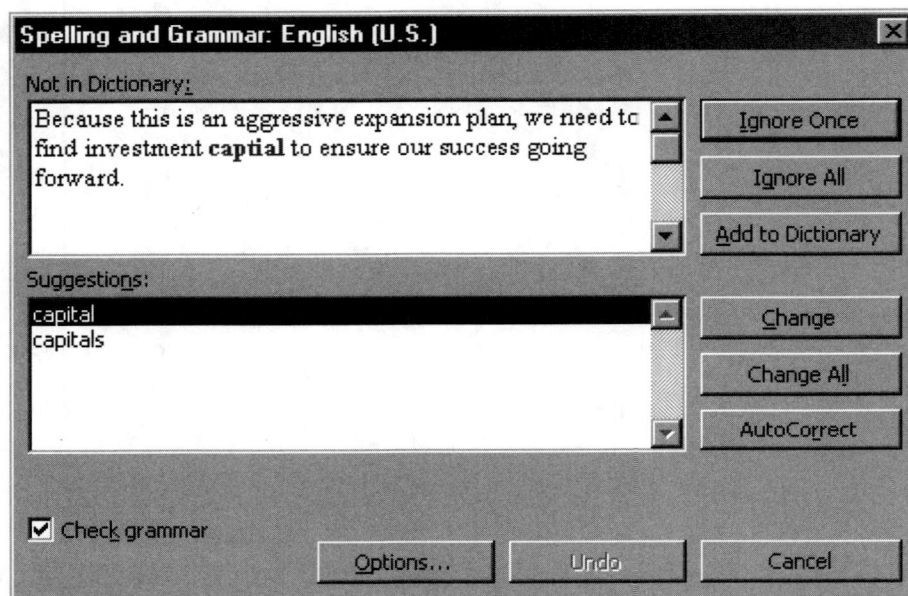

Exhibit 7-1: The Spelling and Grammar dialog box

Note: The default dictionary is the Custom.dic. You can change the dictionary that is used during spell check by clicking the Options button and selecting a new dictionary file from the Custom Dictionary list.

Do it!

A-2: Checking spelling manually

Here's how	Here's why
1 Move to the beginning of the document	
2 Choose **Tools, Spelling and Grammar...**	To open the Spelling and Grammar: English (U.S.) dialog box, as shown in Exhibit 7-1.

3	Observe the Not in Dictionary box	Not in Dictionary: Because this is an aggress find investment **captial** to forward.

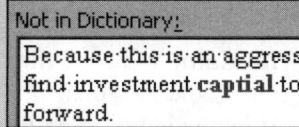

The word "captial" appears in red because Word doesn't recognize the word as a word in its dictionary.

The Suggestions box provides two suggestions for correcting the word "capital," as shown in Exhibit 7-1.

4	Select **capital**	If necessary.
	Click **Change**	To correct the word.
5	Observe the Not in Dictionary box	The misspelled word "porject" appears in red.
	Click **Change**	To correct it with the suggested spelling of "project."
6	Observe the Not in Dictionary box	The misspelled word "porject" appears again.
	Click **Change All**	To correct all occurrences of "porject."
7	Observe the Not in Dictionary box	Word doesn't recognize the proper name "Ann."
	Click **Ignore Once**	To ignore the proper name.
8	Observe the Not in Dictionary box	Word doesn't recognize the proper name "Salinski."
	Click **Ignore Once**	To ignore the proper name.
9	Observe the Not in Dictionary box	The word "Financial" is unrecognized.
	Click **Add to Dictionary**	To add the word to the dictionary so you won't have to correct it again.
10	Ignore any proper names	Microsoft Word ⊠ ⓘ The spelling and grammar check is complete. OK

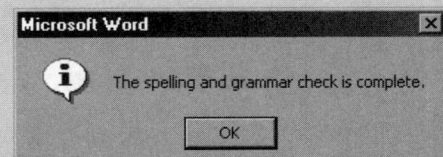

A message box appears, as shown.

11	Click **OK**	To close the message box.
12	Update and close the document	

Checking grammar in a document

Explanation

In addition to checking the spelling, you can use the Spelling and Grammar feature to check the grammar in a document. By default, this option is on when you install Word. When using the Spelling and Grammar dialog box to check grammar, you're prompted for each grammatical error it finds, and you can correct the error. There are times, however, when you might choose not to make the suggested change because what Word sees as an error is an acceptable writing style choice. If you don't understand a grammar rule, click the Help button in the dialog box to read an explanation.

Checking grammar automatically

By default, grammar is checked automatically, and a wavy green line appears under all possible grammatical errors. You can use either the Spelling and Grammar dialog box or the shortcut menu to check grammar. To use the shortcut menu, right-click the word and choose an option from the list.

To open the Spelling and Grammar dialog box, do any of the following:

- Choose Tools, Spelling and Grammar.
- Click the Spelling and Grammar toolbar button.
- Press F7.
- Right-click the word, and choose Grammar to open the Grammar dialog box.

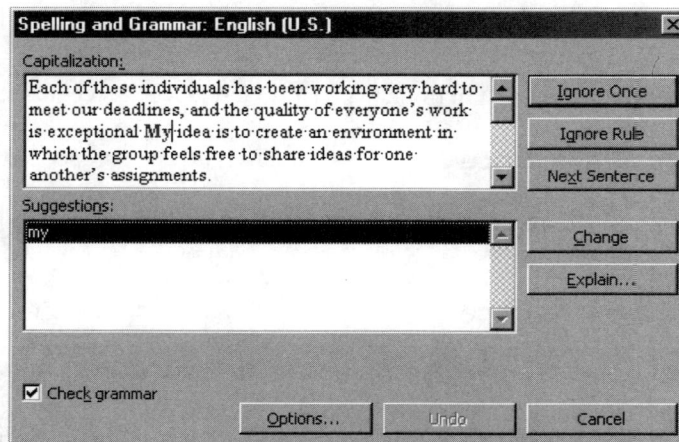

Exhibit 7-2: Checking the grammar

Do it!

A-3:   Checking grammar

Here's how	Here's why
1 Open Grammar	
Save the document as **My grammar**	
2 Click [ABC✓]	(The Spelling and Grammar button is on the Standard toolbar.) To open the Spelling and Grammar dialog box, as shown in Exhibit 7-2.

3 Observe the Capitalization box	Capitalization: Each of these individuals has been working very hard to meet our deadlines, and the quality of everyone's work is exceptional My idea is to create an environment in which the group feels free to share ideas for one another's assignments.
	The word "My" appears in green in the capitalization box because there is a capitalization problem. The problem is due to a missing period after the word "exceptional."
4 Observe the Suggestions box	Word suggests using "my" instead of "My."
5 Click **Explain**	Office Assistant appears with an explanation of when to use capitalization. There are certain words that are always capitalized. The other words should be capitalized only if they appear at the beginning of the sentence.
Click **Explain** again	To close the Office Assistant.
6 In the Capitalization box, click as shown	meet our deadlines and exceptional My idea is
Type a period	The word "My" is no longer green.
7 Click **Next Sentence**	To continue the grammar check.
8 Observe the Punctuation box	Word found a punctuation problem. There are two periods at the end of the sentence.
9 Observe the Suggestions box	There are two suggestions in the box.
Select the second suggestion as shown	Suggestions: . . . ———————— OR — .
Click **Change**	
10 Observe the Extra Space between Words box	Word has found extra spaces between words.
Click **Change**	To delete the extra space between words. A message box appears indicating that the spelling and grammar check is complete.
11 Click **OK**	To close the message box.
Update the document	

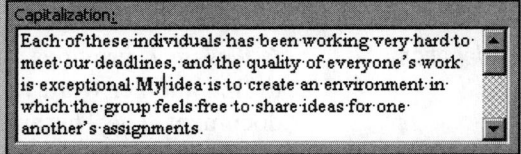

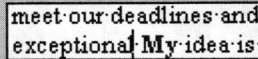

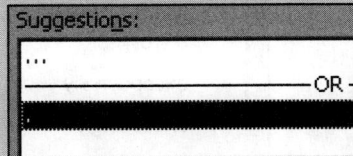

Using the Thesaurus

Explanation
A *thesaurus* provides alternatives, or synonyms, for words. You can use the Thesaurus to find another word with the same or similar meaning to substitute for a word in a document. The Thesaurus provides a list of possible meanings for the selected word, along with a list of synonyms to choose from. If more than one is meaning listed, you can display a list of synonyms for each meaning. You can explore these alternatives further by looking up different meanings for the synonyms provided. Finally, you can also look up an *antonym*, a word with the opposite meaning, in the Thesaurus.

To use the Thesaurus:

1 Select the word for which you want to find an alternative.

2 Choose Tools, Language, Thesaurus. (The first time you use the Language option in the Tools menu, you'll need to click the down chevrons.)

3 Point to the word that you'd like to use.

4 Click the down arrow on the right side of a synonym, and choose Insert to replace the word.

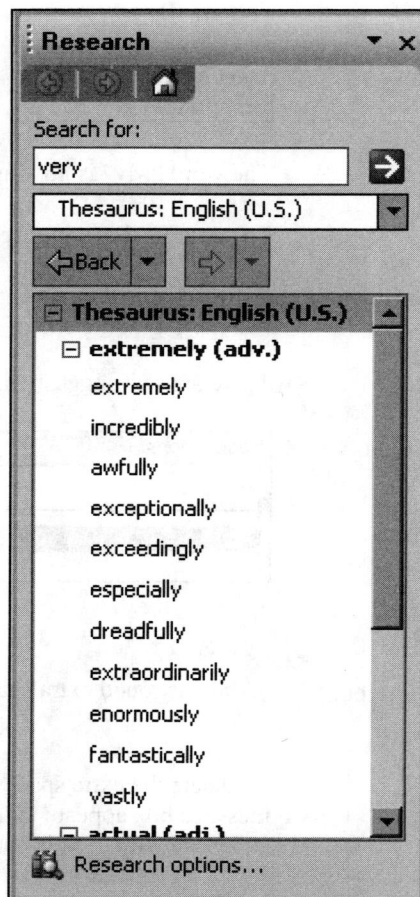

Exhibit 7-3: The Thesaurus: English (U.S.) in the Research task pane

Do it!

A-4: Finding synonyms and antonyms

Here's how	Here's why
1 Select the word **very**	In the first paragraph.
2 Choose **Tools**, **Language**, **Thesaurus…**	To open Thesaurus: English (U.S.). The Thesaurus opens in the Research task pane, as shown in Exhibit 7-3.
3 Observe the Thesaurus: English (U.S.) list	Two meanings for the word "very" and their synonyms are listed.
4 Point as shown	⊟ **actual (adj.)** actual ▼ self-same same
Click the down arrow to the right of "actual"	To display a menu with Insert, Copy, and Look Up commands.
Choose **Look Up**	To display meanings and synonyms for the word "actual."
5 Click **Back**	(The Back button is in the Research task pane.) To return to the lists of meanings and synonyms for the word "very."
6 Display the shortcut menu for **incredibly**	⊟ **extremely (adv.)** extremely incredibly ▼ awfully
	Click the down arrow as shown.
Choose **Insert**	To replace "very" with "incredibly" in the document.
7 In the document, select the word **exceptional**	At the end of the same sentence.
Observe the Search for box	Search for: very ➡
	Even though the Thesaurus is displayed in the task pane, it is still displaying the synonyms for the word "very." You need to activate the Thesaurus again.
Press (SHIFT) + (F7)	To activate the Thesaurus and search for synonyms for the word "exceptional."

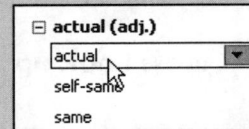

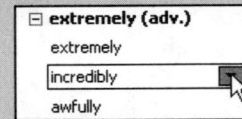

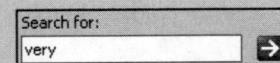

8	Observe the last word in the list	The Thesaurus can be used to find a word's antonym as well.
9	Click as shown	

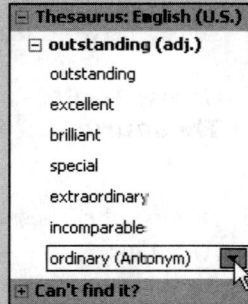

Thesaurus: English (U.S.)
- **outstanding (adj.)**
  - outstanding
  - excellent
  - brilliant
  - special
  - extraordinary
  - incomparable
  - ordinary (Antonym)
- **Can't find it?**

	Choose **Look up**	To see the meanings and synonyms for the word "ordinary."
10	Close the Research task pane	By clicking the Close button in the upper-right corner of the Research task pane.
	Update and close the document	

Topic B: Previewing and printing documents

This topic covers the following Microsoft Office Specialist exam objectives.

#	Objective
WW03S-5-5	Printing documents, envelopes, and labels (This objective is also covered in the Word 2003: Intermediate course in the unit titled "Printing labels and envelopes.")
WW03S-5-6	Previewing a document for printing
WW03S-5-7	Viewing reading layout, normal, outline, full screen, zoom views (This objective is also covered in the unit titled "Editing documents.")

Print Preview

Explanation

The *Print Preview* feature helps you see on the screen what your document will look like when it's printed. By using Print Preview, you can ensure that your document looks the way you want it to before you waste time and effort sending it to the printer.

To preview a document, choose File, Print Preview or click the Print Preview button on the Standard toolbar. The following table describes the Print Preview toolbar buttons.

Button	Name	Used to
	Print	Print a document.
	Magnifier	Show the document in a magnified view. You can increase or decrease the magnification.
	One Page	Show one page at a time in the preview.
	Multiple Pages	Show several pages at a time.
40%	Zoom	View the document at magnification levels ranging from 10 to 400%.
	Full Screen	View documents without any other screen elements—such as the menu bar, the status bar, or the taskbar—present.
	Shrink to Fit	Prevent a small amount of text from flowing onto the last page of the document.
	View Ruler	Show or hide the horizontal ruler. You can use this ruler to set spacing in the document.

Do it!

B-1: Previewing a document

Here's how	Here's why
1 Open **Printing**	From the current unit folder.
Save as **My printing**	
2 Click [icon]	You can also choose File, Print Preview to open the Print Preview window. Your document appears as a reduced version.
3 Display the **Zoom** list	Click the down arrow next to the list.
4 Select **75%**	[dropdown list showing: 40%, 500%, 200%, 150%, 100%, 75%, 50%, 25%, 10%, Page Width, Text Width, Whole Page, Two Pages]
	To display the document at 75% of its original size.
5 Click [icon]	(The Multiple Pages button on the Print Preview toolbar.) You'll select a view for the pages in your document.
6 Select the view as shown	[Multiple pages selector showing 75% and 1 x 2 Pages]
	To view two pages at a time in Print Preview. In the zoom list, the percentage has decreased.
7 Press (PAGE DOWN) several times	To scroll through the document pages in Print Preview.

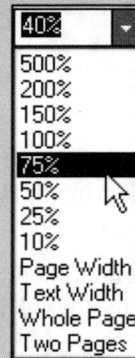

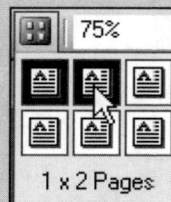

8 Click ▣	(The Full Screen button on the Print Preview toolbar.) To preview the document without any other screen elements. A Full Screen toolbar containing one button appears.
On the Full Screen toolbar, click **Close Full Screen**	To return Print Preview to its normal state.
9 Click **Close**	(The Close button is on the Print Preview toolbar.) To close Print Preview and return to the document area.
10 Click ▣	(The view buttons are on the far left of the horizontal scroll bar, and the Print Layout View button is in the middle of them.) To switch from Normal view to Print Layout view. This view shows you how your document will look when printed.

Printing a document

Explanation

You print a document after you've previewed a document and are satisfied with the way it looks. By default, Word prints one copy of the document. Although you can change the number of copies you send to the printer, keep in mind that it can be less expensive to photocopy a document than to print many copies of it. You can also choose to print a single page or specific pages. You can print a document by clicking the Print button or by choosing File, Print.

The Print button

The Print button (on the Standard toolbar) sends one copy of the current document to your computer's default printer. When you use the Print button, Word uses the default print settings, so you can't specify a page range or change the number of copies printed or the printer to which the document is sent.

The Print dialog box

The Print dialog box provides a number of options you can set when printing a document. You can change the printer the document will print to, print specific pages, print multiple copies, collate multiple pages, print even or odd pages, and use Zoom controls to scale and print multiple pages on one sheet of paper.

Under Page range, you can specify which pages you want to print. For example, to print pages 5 to 10 of a document, enter 5-10 in the Pages box under Page range. You can print multiple copies of a document by specifying a number in the Number of copies box.

To print a document by using the Print dialog box:

1 Choose File, Print or press Ctrl+P.
2 Select and set the options you need in the Print dialog box.
3 Click OK.

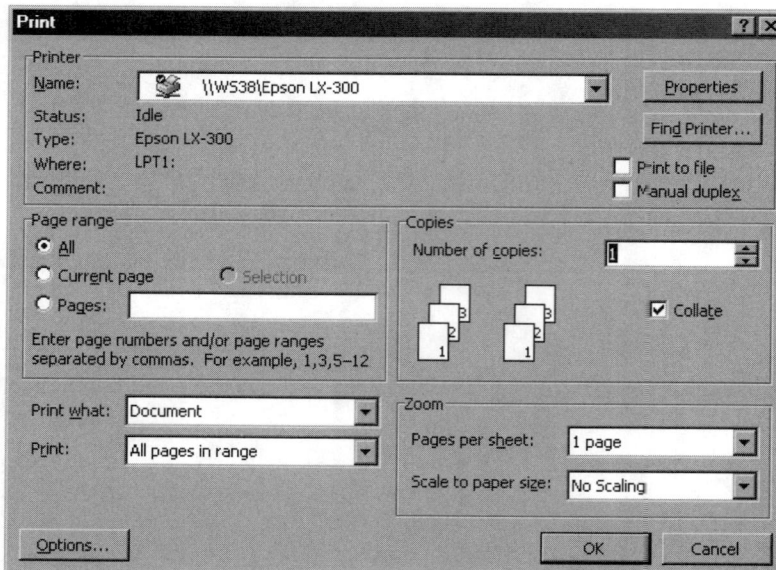

Exhibit 7-4: The Print dialog box

Do it!   **B-2:**   **Using the Print dialog box**

Here's how	Here's why
1 Choose **File**, **Print...**	To open the Print dialog box, as shown in Exhibit 7-4.
Observe the Printer section	You'll see information about the printer to which you're sending the document.
2 Under Page range, in the Pages box, enter **1-2**	To print only pages 1 and 2. (Otherwise, by default, all pages will be printed.) You can also choose to print only the current page.
3 Under Copies, in the Number of copies box, enter **2**	To choose to print two copies. (By default, only one copy is printed and collated.)
4 Display the **Print what** list	

> Document
> ───────────────────
> Document
> Document properties
> Document showing markup
> List of markup
> Styles
> AutoText entries
> Key assignments

(Click the down arrow next to the list.) In addition to printing a document, you can print the document properties, a list of the styles used in the document, and so on.

Close the list	Click the down arrow again or press Esc.
5 Display the **Print** list	

> All pages in range
> ───────────────────
> All pages in range
> Odd pages
> Even pages

You can choose to print all the pages, the odd pages, or the even pages of a document.

Close the list	
6 Click **OK**	To print the current document. If your computer is not connected to a printer, click Cancel instead.
Update and close the document	

Unit summary: Proofing and printing documents

Topic A In this topic, you learned how to locate and correct misspelled words by using Word's **spelling checker** to check spelling both automatically and manually. You also used the grammar checker to check grammar in a document. In addition, you learned how to use the **Thesaurus** to find synonyms and antonyms for words.

Topic B In this topic, you learned how to preview a document before printing it by clicking the **Print Preview** button on the Standard toolbar. In addition, you printed a document by using the Print button and the **Print** dialog box.

Independent practice activity

1 Open Final and save it as **My Final**.

2 Correct the spelling and grammar in the document.

3 Select the word "initial" in the fourth bullet.

4 Use the Thesaurus to replace the word "initial" with a word of your choice.

5 Preview and print the document. (You don't need to print if you aren't set up to do so.)

6 Close the Research task pane.

7 Update and close the document.

Review questions

1 What does automatic spell check mode mean?

2 What are the ways to manually check the spelling?

3 How does Word indicate a grammar error?

A A wavy red underline

B A dot in the left margin

C A solid green underline

D A wavy green underline

4 Which buttons in Print Preview enable you to change the magnification of the document?

5 What does the Full Screen button in Print Preview do?

6 When you click the Print button on the Standard toolbar, what is printed?

7 What should you do if you want to print only selected pages?

Unit 8

Web features

Unit time: 30 minutes

Complete this unit, and you'll know how to:

A Save and open a document as a Web page.

B Insert and use hyperlinks in a document.

C Send a document via e-mail.

Topic A: Saving documents as Web pages

This topic covers the following Microsoft Office Specialist exam objectives.

#	Objective
WW03S-5-4	Saving documents as Web pages
WW03S-5-6	Previewing a Web page for publication
WW03E-4-2	Setting Web options and saving to a Web server

Web Layout view

Explanation

A *Web browser* is software used to access Web sites, which contain Web pages. Each Web page contains code in *Hypertext Markup Language (HTML)*. Even if you're not familiar with HTML, you can design and create a Web page by using the advanced formatting and editing features of Word. You save a Word document as a Web page by choosing File, Save as Web Page.

While creating a Web page in Word, you might want to see how the file will look when published to the Web. To do this, you can use Web Layout view in Word. In this view, you can see backgrounds, formatting, and other effects, as they'll appear when viewed online.

To switch to Web Layout view, choose View, Web Layout. You can also click the Web Layout View button, placed to the left of the horizontal scrollbar.

In addition to Web Layout view, you can see how your document will look in a Web browser by choosing File, Web Page Preview. When you do this, a copy of your document is saved and then opened in your default browser. After previewing the document, close the browser window to return to your document in Word.

Do it!

A-1: Previewing a document as a Web page

Here's how	Here's why
1 Open About us	(From the current unit folder.) You'll view this document in Web Layout view and then preview this document as a Web page.
2 Choose **View, Web Layout**	To view the document in Web Layout view. The document now appears as it would in a browser window.
3 Choose **File, Web Page Preview**	The document is saved and opened in your Web browser.
Observe the title bar	The default page title is the document path.
4 Maximize the browser window	If necessary.
5 Close the browser window	To return to your document in Word.

Using the Save as Web page command

Explanation

You save a Word document as a Web page by choosing File, Save as Web Page. You'll notice that the Save As dialog box is opened, but the file type is a Web page.

By default, the file is saved as a single-file Web page with the extension .mht. When you save the document as a Single File Web Page, the graphics and images in the document are embedded in the Web page.

You can also save the file as a regular Web page. In this case, the file is saved as an HTML document with the extension .htm, and all the graphics and images in the document are saved in an associated folder. Although the HTML file is smaller, it's easier to e-mail the MHTML file because all of the supporting graphic files are included.

The HTML format might not support all the Word formatting used in a document. When you've saved a document as a Web page, a warning appears if the formatting in the document cannot be saved in HTML format.

Changing the page title

In Web pages, the title bar usually contains descriptive text for the Web page. For example, the title bar for www.course.com contains "Course Technology – Leading the Way in IT Publishing." The title does not need to be long, but it should be descriptive.

To enter a new page title:

1 Choose File, Save As Web Page.
2 Click Change Title to open the Set Page Title dialog box.
3 Enter a descriptive title and click OK.
4 Verify that the file name is correct.
5 Click Save to save the Web page with a new page title.

Web options

The Web Options dialog box contains a variety of settings that can be used to tailor the document to your Web audience. For example, you can disable features that are not supported by certain browsers.

To change Web option settings, choose Tools, Options and click the Web Options button. Each tab in the Web Options dialog box contains settings that you can modify. To continue with the previous example, click the Browsers tab and choose the category of Web browsers that people will be using. Then, check "Disable features not supported by these browsers."

Saving to a Web server

In addition to saving your Web pages on your local hard drive or in a network folder, you might want to save the Web page directly to a Web server. To do so, you must have the appropriate rights to save files on the Web server. You will also need to know the URL, or Web address, for the Web server.

To save a Web page to a Web server:

1 Choose File, Save as Web Page. (Or, choose File, Save As to save a file.)
2 In the File name box, enter the Web server's URL, path to the file (optional), and a file name. For example, to save Doc1 on www.mysite.com, enter the following: `www.mysite.com/Doc1`
3 If necessary, select the desired folder.
4 Click Save.

Do it!

A-2:   Saving a document as a Web page

Here's how	Here's why
1 Verify that Word is maximized, with the file About us shown in the document area	You'll save this document as a Web page.
2 Choose **File, Save As Web Page...**	To open the Save As dialog box.
3 In the File name box, enter **My about us**	To name the file.
4 In the Save as type, select **Web Page**	To save the document as a Web page with the .htm extension.
5 Click **Change Title**	(The Change Title button is above the File name box.) To open the Set Page Title dialog box.
In the Page title box, enter **About Outlander Spices**	This title will appear in the title bar of the browser when you open this Web page.
Click **OK**	Page title: About Outlander Spices
	To close the Set Page Title dialog box. The title appears above the File name box.
6 Click **Save**	To save the file and close the Save As dialog box. The New Blank Document button on the Standard toolbar is replaced by the New Web Page button.
7 Close the document	
8 Open Windows Explorer	
Navigate to the current unit folder in Student Data	
Observe the contents of the folder My about us_files	This folder contains five image files and a file list document used to display this HTML document.
Close Windows Explorer	

Opening HTML documents in a browser

Explanation To open an HTML document in a browser:

1 Click Start and choose Programs, Internet Explorer. (You can also double-click the Internet Explorer icon on the desktop.)

2 Choose File, Open to browse for a file. (You can also open a file in a browser by entering the address of the Web page in the Address box and pressing Enter.)

3 Select the file.

4 Click Open.

5 Click OK.

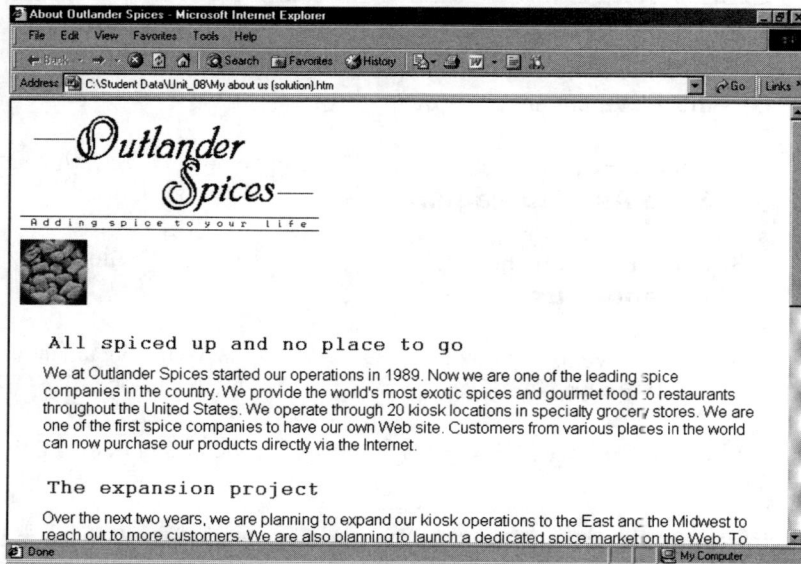

Exhibit 8-1: The Web page opened in Internet Explorer

Do it!   **A-3: Opening an HTML document in a browser**

Here's how	Here's why
1 Choose **Start**, **Programs**, **Internet Explorer**	To start Internet Explorer.
2 Choose **File**, **Open…**	The Open dialog box appears.
Click **Browse**	To open the Microsoft Internet Explorer dialog box.
Select **My about us**	From the current unit folder.
Click **Open**	To close the Microsoft Internet Explorer dialog box. The path for the My about us document appears in the Open dialog box.
Click **OK**	To open the file in the browser window, as shown in Exhibit 8-1. The Web page resembles how it looked in Web Page Preview in Word.
3 Observe the page title	It displays the text you entered in the Page title box: About Outlander Spices.
4 Close Internet Explorer	Choose File, Close.

Opening an HTML document in Word for editing

Explanation

When you need to change an HTML document, you can open the .htm file in Word for editing. To do so:

1 Choose File, Open.

2 Select the HTML document in the list of files.

3 Click Open.

4 Modify the document as necessary, and save the file. The file will automatically be resaved as an HTML document.

If you're using Microsoft Internet Explorer, you can also choose File, Edit in Microsoft Word for Windows from the browser window. The file will be opened in Word.

Opening HTML documents created in other Office applications

When you select an HTML document to open by using the Open dialog box, the file will be opened in the application that the file was created in. For example, if the file was created in Excel, the file will open in Excel. To open an HTML file created in another Office application in Word:

1 Choose File, Open.

2 Right-click the HTML document to display the shortcut menu.

3 Choose Open in Microsoft Word.

Do it!

A-4:   Opening an HTML document in Word

Here's how	Here's why
1 Open My about us	This is the Word document that you recently saved as a Web page.
2 Place the insertion point as shown	` ··All·spiced ` ` We·at·Outlander·Spic `
	You'll edit the document.
Type **Welcome to Outlander Spices!** Press (SPACEBAR)	
3 Select the paragraph under the heading "All spiced up and no place to go"	You'll apply the format of this paragraph to the paragraphs under the heading "Our products."
Double-click 🖌	To use the Format Painter button to copy the formatting to more than one paragraph.
4 Apply the format to the paragraph under "Our products"	By using the Format Painter tool, select the paragraph.
5 Apply the same format to the paragraph under "Our progress to date"	
6 Click 🖌	To turn off the Format Painter tool.
Deselect the text	
7 Choose **File**, **Save**	To save the file. The file will automatically be saved as an HTML document.
8 Choose **File**, **Web Page Preview**	To preview the changes you made to the file.
Close the browser window	

Topic B: Working with hyperlinks

This topic covers the following Microsoft Office Specialist exam objective.

#	Objective
WW03S-2-3	Inserting and modifying hyperlinks to other documents and Web pages

Inserting hyperlinks in a document

Explanation

Hyperlinks are words or graphics that are used to navigate the Web. A hyperlink can lead you to another location on the same Web page or to another Web page.

When you point to a hyperlink, the shape of the pointer changes to a hand, and a ScreenTip appears. By default, the hyperlink is blue and underlined.

You can insert hyperlinks in a document by choosing Insert, Hyperlink or by clicking the Insert Hyperlink button on the Standard toolbar.

To insert a hyperlink in a document:

1 Select the text that you want to make a hyperlink.
2 Choose Insert, Hyperlink to open the Insert Hyperlink dialog box.
3 Use the ScreenTip button to specify a ScreenTip for the hyperlink.
4 In the address box, enter the location of the HTML file, document, or other file to which you want to link.
5 Click OK.

Do it!

B-1:   Inserting a hyperlink

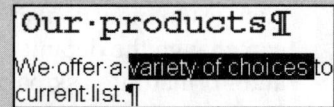

Here's how	Here's why
1 Scroll down to see the picture and text at the bottom of the page	If necessary.
2 Select **variety of choices**	Our·products¶ We·offer·a·variety·of·choices·to current·list.¶
	(Under the heading "Our products.") You'll make this text a hyperlink.
3 Choose **Insert, Hyperlink...**	To open the Insert Hyperlink dialog box.
4 Click **ScreenTip**	To open the Set Hyperlink ScreenTip dialog box. You'll create a custom ScreenTip for your hyperlink to provide users with more information.
In the ScreenTip box, enter **To learn more about our product line.**	
Click **OK**	To close the dialog box.
5 In the File list, select **Our products**	Browsed Pages My about us / Our products / Our sales / Team Recent Files Address: Our products.htm
	To create a hyperlink to the HTML file, Our products. As soon as you select Our products, the file name appears in the Address box (Our products.htm).
Click **OK**	To create the hyperlink. The text "variety of choices" appears blue and underlined, indicating that it's a hyperlink.

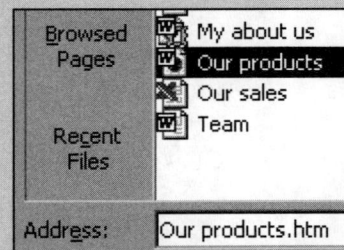

Using hyperlinks

Explanation

You can use hyperlinks to navigate to the linked files. When you click a hyperlink, the mouse pointer must be in the shape of a pointing finger. To use a hyperlink in Word, press and hold Ctrl, and then click the hyperlink.

The linked file will open in its source application. After you click a hyperlink, the color changes to indicate that it has been used. This is known as a *followed hyperlink*. You can change the default colors of hyperlinks and followed hyperlinks by using the Styles and Formatting task pane.

Do it!

B-2: Navigating with hyperlinks

Here's how	Here's why
1 Point to the hyperlink	products¶ To learn more about our product line. **CTRL + click to follow link** r·a·variety·of·choices·to·our·customers·and·we The custom ScreenTip you created appears. A message on how to access the link also appears.
2 Press and hold CTRL	We·offer·a·variety·of·choices·to· current·list.¶ The mouse pointer changes to a pointing finger, indicating that this is a hyperlink.
Click the hyperlink	To open Our products.htm in Internet Explorer.
Release CTRL	
3 Click **Back** as shown	⇐ Back ▾ → ▾ ⊗ ↻ Address ⋯ Back to My about us (The Back button is on the Browser toolbar.) To go back to the Word document. The hyperlink changes color, indicating that you've followed the link.

Hyperlinks to an Excel file

Explanation

You can create hyperlinks to a Web page, a Word document, or other types of files. For example, you might want to open an Excel file from a Word document. To do this, you can create a hyperlink to the Excel file in your Word document.

The Web toolbar also helps you navigate between documents.

Do it!

B-3: Creating a hyperlink to Excel

Here's how	Here's why
1 Select **yearly sales data**	(Under the heading "Our progress to date.") You'll make this a hyperlink to an Excel file that contains sales data.
2 Open the Insert Hyperlink dialog box	Choose Insert, Hyperlink, or right-click and choose Hyperlink from the shortcut menu.
Select **Our sales**	(In the current unit folder.) This is an Excel file.
Click **OK**	To close the dialog box.
3 Observe the hyperlink ScreenTip	The default ScreenTip displays the file name and path of the linked file.
4 Press (CTRL) and click the hyperlink	

The yearly sales report appears. The Web toolbar appears in the Excel window.

5 Close Excel	
6 Update and close My About us	

Topic C: E-mailing documents

This topic covers the following Microsoft Office Specialist exam objectives.

#	Objective
WW03S-4-1	Sending documents for review via e-mail
WW03S-4-1	Sending documents in an e-mail or as an e-mail attachment

Sending documents through e-mail

Explanation

As you work in Word and other Office applications, you might need to send a document you've created to another person via e-mail. To do this, you and the recipient should have both Word and an e-mail program installed.

To send a Word document via e-mail, you must have Word 2003 and an e-mail program installed on your computer. Depending on the e-mail program you're using, the available e-mail features and options might vary. When you attach a Word 2003 document, the recipient must have Word 2000 or later to view the attachment. If the recipient can't view the attachment, you might need to save the file as a different type.

To send a document via e-mail:

1 Open the document you want to send.
2 Choose File, Send to, Mail Recipient (as Attachment). A message window opens with the document attached.
3 Enter or select the recipient's e-mail address, and enter any message you want to include.
4 Click Send.

Do it!   **C-1:   Sending documents via e-mail**

Questions and answers

1 What two applications do you need to have installed to send Word 2003 documents via e-mail?

2 What applications does your recipient need to have installed to view the document you're sending?

3 What are the basic steps you follow to send a document to someone via e-mail?

Unit summary: Web features

Topic A
In this topic, you learned how to preview a document as a Web page and how to **save a Word document as an HTML file**. You previewed a document by using the **Web Page Preview** command. In addition, you opened the HTML file in a Web browser to see how the file will look online.

Topic B
In this topic, you learned how to insert a **hyperlink** and how to use the hyperlink to move to the linked file. You also inserted hyperlinks to other files, such as Excel files.

Topic C
In this topic, you learned how to **send a document via e-mail**. You learned that to send a document via e-mail, you need Word 2003 and an e-mail program installed on your computer.

Independent practice activity

1 Open Team.

2 Preview the document as a Web page. Close the browser.

3 Save the file as a Single File Web Page, and name it **My team**.

4 Open My team in Internet Explorer.

5 Close Internet Explorer.

6 At the bottom of the page, make the text **Back to previous page** a hyperlink to the file **My about us.htm**.

7 Click the hyperlink to display the HTML file.

8 Close Internet Explorer.

9 Update and close the document.

10 Open Windows Explorer and navigate to the current unit folder to view My team. Is there a folder named My team_files? If not, why not?

11 Close Word and Windows Explorer.

Review questions

1 What is the command to save a Word document as a Web page?

2 How can you check the appearance of your Web page before you save or publish it?

3 How do you change the Web options?

4 Which of the following is not necessary to save a file to a Web server?

   A Server URL

   B Page title

   C Appropriate rights and access to the Web server

   D File name

5 Once a hyperlink has been followed, does anything change?

6 Describe the procedure for inserting a hyperlink in a document.

7 If you attach a Word 2003 document to an e-mail and the recipient cannot view the attachment, what should you do?

Appendix A

Instant Messaging

This appendix covers this additional topic:

A Using Instant Messaging.

Topic A: Instant Messaging

Explanation

By using the *Instant Messaging* feature of Office 2003, you can send and receive messages instantly over the Internet or an intranet. This can be significantly faster than e-mail communication, in which messages are not received until they are downloaded from a server.

To send and receive instant messages, you use one of several *instant messengers*, which are stand-alone programs that you can download and install. One example of an instant messenger is MSN Messenger (shown in Exhibit A-1).

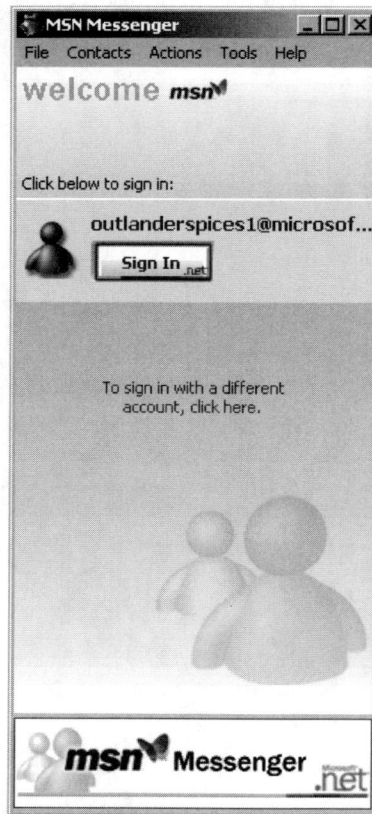

Exhibit A-1: The MSN Messenger sign-in window

Instant messaging in Word

In Word, a Person Names smart tag indicates the online status of a contact. Online status information is available only for people whose instant messaging addresses you have added to your instant messaging contact list.

When you type the e-mail address of an instant messaging contact in Word, the Person Names smart tag will appear. If the smart tag indicates that the contact is online, you can select the name and initiate a conversation. However, if the contact is offline, you will not be able to communicate with that person.

Instant messaging technologies

You can implement Instant Messaging in your Office applications by using any of the following technologies:

- **MSN Messenger Service** — An application for sending and receiving instant messages.
- **NetMeeting** — Enables you to participate in meetings over the Internet or an intranet.
- **SharePoint Services** — Enables aggregation, collaboration, and search capabilities for people, teams, and information.
- **Microsoft Live Communication Server** — An extensible platform that can deliver presence capabilities and instant messaging services through familiar user interfaces.

Enabling Instant Messaging

To send instant messages in Word, Person Name smart tags must be enabled. To verify this:

1 Start Word.
2 Choose Tools, AutoCorrect Options to open the AutoCorrect dialog box.
3 Activate the Smart Tags tab (as shown in Exhibit A-2).
4 Under Recognizers, verify that the following options are checked:
   - Person Name (English)
   - Person Name (Outlook e-mail recipients)
5 Click OK.

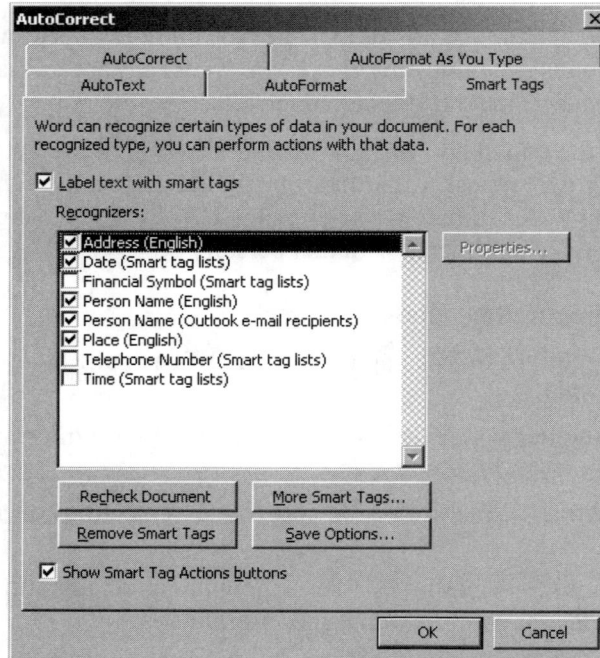

Exhibit A-2: The Smart Tags tab of the AutoCorrect dialog box

Sending instant messages

Word uses MSN Messenger to send instant messages. Before you can send an instant message, the recipient must be in your contact list, and both of you must be online. After adding the recipient to your contact list, it is recommended that you restart Word and the messenger application. To start an instant message, click the Person Name smart tag to display the shortcut menu, and then choose Send Instant Message.

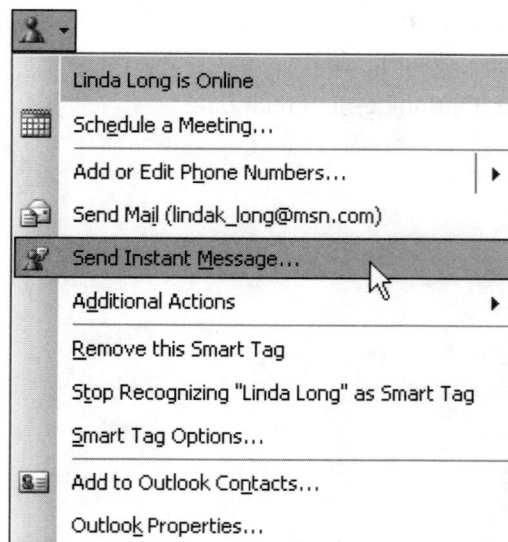

Exhibit A-3: The shortcut menu used to send instant messages

If you are using MSN Messenger, you will see a window like the one shown in Exhibit A-4. Simply type a message at the bottom of the window and click Send. The recipient will receive your message instantly.

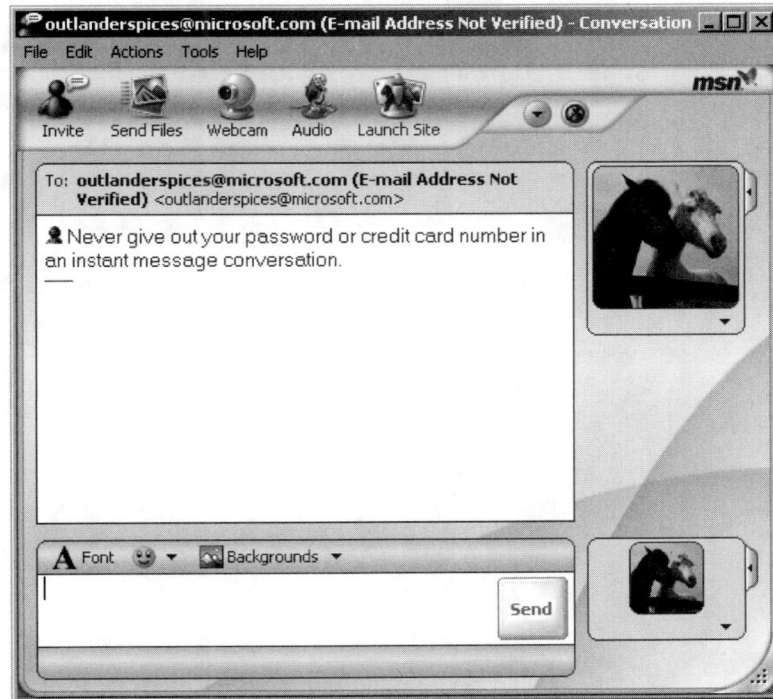

Exhibit A-4: Using MSN Messenger to send an instant message

Appendix B

Alternative user input

This appendix covers these additional topics:

A Speech recognition.

B Handwriting recognition.

C Using Office Document Imaging to import scanned text into Word.

Topic A: Speech recognition

Explanation

You've probably seen science fiction films or TV shows in which people use their voices to communicate with computers. This is no longer a futuristic vision. With Office 2003's speech recognition feature, you can control Word 2003 by speaking into a microphone. You can also use this feature to access menu commands, select options, scroll through a document, "click" buttons, and so on.

Preparation

Before you start using speech recognition with Word, there are two operational factors to consider. First, the speech recognition feature is not designed for completely hands-free operation. You'll get the best results if you use a combination of your voice and the mouse or keyboard. Second, speech recognition works best in a quiet setting. If your work environment has a significant amount of background noise, then you might have some difficulty communicating with your computer through a microphone.

Microphones and other system requirements

Even if you work in a quiet office, you need to ensure that your computer is equipped with the proper hardware and software. First, you'll need a high-quality close-talk microphone, also called a *headset microphone. Close-talk microphones* remain at a constant distance from your mouth. After the microphone has been positioned properly, the headset will keep it there no matter how you move your head.

Before you install the speech recognition feature, you should also make sure that your system has all of the following:

- 400 megahertz (MHz) or faster processor
- At least 128 MB RAM
- Windows 2000 or later
- Internet Explorer 5 or later

Getting started

A typical, default installation of Office 2003 does not include the speech recognition feature. There are two ways to add this feature after Office 2003 has been installed. First, you can trigger installation by starting Word and choosing Tools, Speech. You'll be prompted to insert the Office 2003 installation CD, after which you simply follow the instructions on your screen.

The other alternative is to run the setup program on the CD and select the Add or Remove Features option. You'll find Speech under Office Shared Features, Alternative User Input. (You can also do this as part of a custom installation of Office 2003.)

Voice training

To start using speech recognition, choose Tools, Speech. The first time you do this, you'll be prompted to complete a process called *voice training*. During voice training, the computer learns to recognize your voice by "listening" to you read a series of text passages displayed on screen. As you speak, the Voice Training wizard indicates that it has "understood" you by highlighting each word in succession, as shown in Exhibit B-1.

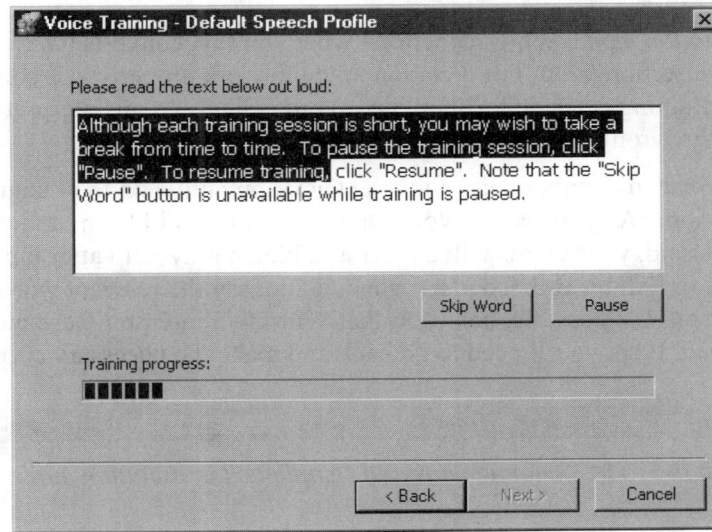

Exhibit B-1: The Voice Training – Default Speech Profile dialog box

This procedure, which takes about 15 minutes, will also help you feel more comfortable with the headset, speak at the suitable volume and speed, and position your microphone properly. The ideal microphone position is about an inch, or a thumb's width, to the side of your mouth. The microphone should not be directly in front of your mouth, and you should avoid breathing directly into it.

Introducing the Language bar

After you've completed the initial voice training procedure, the Language bar (as shown in Exhibit B-2) will appear in the upper-right corner of the Word window. This toolbar is your primary on-screen tool for working with speech recognition. The toolbar is floating, so you can position it anywhere you want. You can control the Language bar with your voice or your mouse.

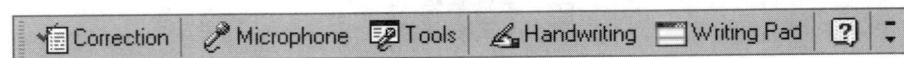

Exhibit B-2: The Language bar

To turn on speech recognition, click the Microphone button on the Language bar. The button will be selected to indicate that the computer is "listening." To turn off speech recognition, you can click the Microphone button again, or you can simply say "microphone."

When speech recognition is turned on, the Language bar also indicates which recognition mode is selected: dictation or voice command. You'll learn about these two modes in the following sections.

When you're not using speech recognition, you can close or minimize the Language bar. To close the bar, right-click it to display the shortcut menu, and then choose Close the Language bar. To redisplay the bar, choose Tools, Speech.

To minimize the Language bar, click the minus sign (-) in the upper-right corner of the bar. When you do so, the Language bar icon (with the letters "EN," for English) will appear on the taskbar next to the clock. To restore the Language bar, click the icon and then choose Show the Language bar.

Dictation mode

In *dictation mode*, Word recognizes what you say, converts it to text, and enters that text at the insertion point. For dictation mode to work properly and consistently, thorough voice training is needed. Otherwise, Word is likely to misinterpret what you say and enter the wrong text.

To activate dictation mode, click the Dictation button on the Language bar, or say "dictation." As you speak, Word types. If Word is still trying to interpret something you've said, your words will appear as a bluish gray strip after the last typed word, as shown in Exhibit B-3. To insert punctuation, say the relevant word: "period," "comma," and so on. It's possible, however, that Word will interpret these utterances as words to be typed. If so, you'll need to go back and make the necessary corrections.

Exhibit B-3: The Language bar and sample text in dictation mode

Making corrections

When you use dictation mode, it's inevitable that Word will misinterpret some words or phrases. This is due partly to the limitations of current speech recognition technology and partly to the fact that different words can sound identical, such as "there," "their," and "they're."

The simplest way to make corrections is with your keyboard and mouse, both of which remain active as you dictate. You can also use the Correction button on the Language bar. You can click this button with your mouse or "click" with your voice by saying "correction." When you do so, Word will play a recording of the last word you said, select that word, and display a list of alternatives, as shown in Exhibit B-4. To replace the selected word, just click the correct alternative. You can also say "next" to move down the list; when you get to the correct alternative, say "select" to insert it.

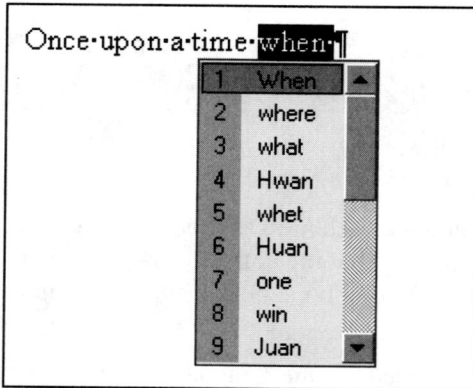

Exhibit B-4: Making corrections by using the Language bar

Voice command mode

In *voice command mode*, you use your voice to access menu commands, "click" buttons, select options, and so on. In this mode, you can use your voice to perform actions that you normally do by using the mouse.

To activate voice command mode, click the Voice Command button on the Language bar, or say "voice command." After that, the words you say will be interpreted as commands rather than dictated text, and each understood command will be displayed on the Language bar. For example, to display the File menu, say "file." You're not limited to the first-level menus, however. You can go deeper into a menu by saying each word in succession. So, to open the Insert Table dialog box, say "table, insert, table," pausing briefly between words. In the dialog box, you can use your voice to select options, and "click" buttons by simply saying their names.

You can also use voice commands to scroll through a document. For example, you can say "home" to move the insertion point to the beginning of a line, or say "go end" to move to the end of a line. To scroll down one page, say "page down," and to scroll up one page, say "page up."

The following table lists several other voice commands:

Say this...	To do this...
"New document" or "New blank document"	Create a new, blank document
"Expand" or "More buttons"	Display all of the commands in a menu
"Tab" / "Shift tab"	In a dialog box, move to the next or previous option
"Return" or "Enter" or "New line"	Enter a new line (same as pressing the Enter key)
"Select all"	Select the entire document
"Select next word" or "Shift control right"	Select the next word
"Select last word" or "Shift control left"	Select the previous word
"Italicize" or "Italics"	Apply and remove italics
"On bold" or "Begin bolding"	Apply bold text formatting
"Undo" / "Redo"	Undo or redo the previous action
"Cut" / "Copy" / "Paste"	Cut, copy, or paste the selected item
"Ask a question" or "Type a question for help"	Move the insertion point to the Ask a Question box
"Escape" or "Cancel"	Close a menu, or close a dialog box without saving changes

Troubleshooting

If you experience problems while using the speech recognition feature, here are some things you can do:

- Conduct additional voice training—the more, the better. To do this, click the Tools button on the Language bar, and then choose Training.

- Check your microphone to make sure that it's working properly and that it's in the correct position. You might even need to get a better microphone.

- Eliminate as much background noise as possible.

- Speak in a consistent, level tone. Speaking too loudly or too softly makes it difficult for the computer to recognize what you've said.

- When dictating text, speak without pausing between words; a phrase is easier for the computer to interpret than just one word. Also, pronounce words clearly, but don't separate or overemphasize each syllable in a word.

- If a voice command does not appear to work, switch to another program, switch back to the program you were working in, and then say the command again. If the command does not work as expected by the third or fourth try, do not continue to repeat the command. Instead, use your mouse or keyboard.

- For additional assistance, consult Word's online Help system.

Topic B: Handwriting recognition

Explanation If you're not comfortable with using the keyboard, you might want to try Office 2003's handwriting recognition feature. Using your mouse or a special input device, you can write out your text in longhand, and Word will convert it into typed text. This feature is also useful for creating simulated signatures.

Handwriting input devices

To use handwriting recognition to enter text in Word, you don't need any special accessories. That is, you can use your mouse to simulate the act of writing by hand. However, you'll probably find it more comfortable to work with some sort of tablet device. Commonly used with graphics programs, a *tablet* system consists of a flat, electronically sensitive input surface and a pen-like stylus device. You use the stylus to write on the tablet the same way you would use a pencil to write on a sheet of paper. Before you install a tablet system for the purpose of handwriting recognition, you should make sure that the tablet is compatible with Office 2003.

Installation

A typical default installation of Office 2003 does not include the handwriting recognition feature. If Office 2003 is already installed, run the setup program from the CD, and select Add or Remove Features. You'll find Handwriting under Office Shared Features, Alternative User Input.

You can also include handwriting recognition as part of Office 2003's initial setup by performing a custom installation.

Getting started

After you install the handwriting recognition feature, the Language bar will appear automatically when you start Word. Use the buttons on the Language bar to turn handwriting recognition on and off, change your handwriting settings, and make corrections.

Text mode vs. ink mode

Before you start working with the Language bar and handwriting recognition, it's important to understand the difference between the two recognition modes: text mode and ink mode.

In *text mode*, whatever you write is converted into typed text and entered in the document at the insertion point. This is the most common application of handwriting recognition.

In *ink mode*, Word turns your handwriting into graphics called *ink objects*. You can think of ink objects as small drawings that look exactly like your own handwriting. For this reason, ink mode is used to create simulated signatures. After the object is inserted, you can format an ink object in the same way that you would format typed text. For example, you can make an ink object bigger by applying a larger point size, or you can make it stand out on the page by applying bold formatting or a different color.

Finally, you can convert an ink object to typed text by right-clicking the object to display the shortcut menu and choosing Ink Object, Recognize.

The Writing Pad

The Writing Pad is a separate window in which you write the text to be inserted into your document. You activate the Writing Pad by clicking the Handwriting button on the Language bar (to display the Handwriting menu) and then choosing Writing Pad. It's a good idea to position the Writing Pad so that it doesn't obscure your view of the text as it's inserted in the document.

When you point to the writing area, the mouse pointer changes to a pen, as shown in Exhibit B-5. The horizontal line in the writing area can help you keep your writing straight and neat, thus making it easier for Word to interpret the text correctly. Outside of the writing area, the mouse will function normally.

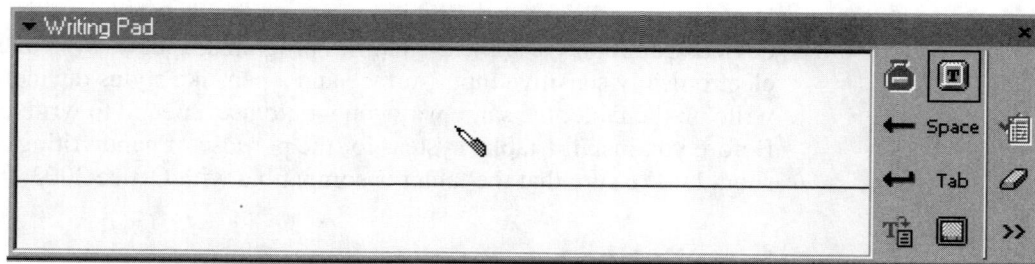

Exhibit B-5: The pen in the Writing Pad

On the right side of the Writing Pad, you'll find a collection of buttons. The following table describes the function of each button:

Button	What it does
	Enters text in handwritten format
	Activates text mode (permanently selected)
	Displays the on-screen standard keyboard, which you can use the same way as a regular keyboard, except that you click the keys with the mouse
	Activates the Drawing Pad
	Deletes the previous character or the contents of the selected word (same as pressing the Backspace key)
	Enters the current text and moves down one line (same as pressing the Enter key)
Space	Inserts a space (same as pressing the spacebar)
Tab	Moves one tab space to the right (same as pressing the Tab key)
	Moves one line up or down or one character left or right (same as pressing the arrow keys)
	Triggers Word to convert what you have written in the writing area (if Word is not set up for automatic recognition)
	Switches to Write Anywhere mode (explained later in this topic)
	Enables you to correct errors in the Writing Pad when Word misinterprets your handwriting or when you type something incorrectly
	Clears the contents of the writing area
« or »	Expands or reduces the number of buttons shown on the Writing Pad

About automatic recognition

By default, Word converts your handwriting automatically as you write. This automatic conversion occurs whenever you pause between numbers or words. Even if you leave spaces between words, Word will not convert the text until you actually stop writing for a moment. Any spaces you leave between words will be entered as space characters in the document.

Sometimes, you might want to turn off automatic recognition. To do so, use the Handwriting Options dialog box, as shown in Exhibit B-6. Here's how:

1 Click the down arrow in the top-left corner of the Writing Pad to display the Writing Pad menu.

2 Choose Options to open the Handwriting Options dialog box. By default, the Common tab is activated.

3 Clear Automatic recognition.

4 Click OK.

By turning off automatic recognition, you give yourself a chance to examine what you've written before it's converted and entered in the document.

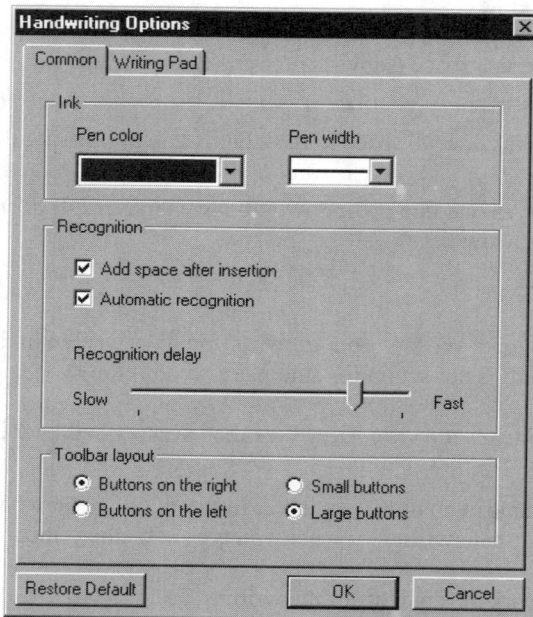

Exhibit B-6: The Handwriting Options dialog box

Making corrections

If Word has misinterpreted something you wrote on the Writing Pad, you can correct the error by selecting it (with the mouse or keyboard) and rewriting the correct text. Of course, you can also enter the correct text by typing it with the keyboard.

Turning off handwriting recognition

When you want to stop using handwriting recognition, close the Writing Pad by clicking the Writing Pad button on the Language bar or by clicking the Close button in the upper-right corner of the Writing Pad.

Write Anywhere

If you don't want to use the Writing Pad, you can work in Write Anywhere mode. To activate this mode, display the Handwriting menu (on the Language bar) and choose Write Anywhere. In this mode, you can write anywhere on the screen. (You're not writing directly on your monitor, of course; you're still using your mouse or your tablet system.) The floating Write Anywhere toolbar provides the same buttons as the Writing Pad, and most of the procedures are the same. In Write Anywhere mode, however, you cannot use the mouse to drag the scrollbars. To do this, you must switch to the Writing Pad or turn off handwriting recognition.

Switching to the Writing Pad

To switch from Write Anywhere mode to the Writing Pad, click the Writing Pad button on the Write Anywhere toolbar, or choose Writing Pad from the Handwriting menu.

Turning off handwriting recognition

In Write Anywhere mode, when you want to stop using handwriting recognition, click the Write Anywhere button on the Language bar, or click the Close button in the upper-right corner of the Write Anywhere toolbar.

Topic C: Working with Office Document Imaging

Explanation

Suppose you've received a copy of a manuscript, and you want to re-create it in Word. If the original document is not available in electronic form, you can scan the pages and then use the Office Document Imaging program to send the scanned document to Word as typed text.

About TIFF files

Most scanning programs give you the option of saving scanned files in several formats, such as bitmap (.bmp) or TIFF (.tif). TIFF, which stands for *Tagged Image File Format*, is the only format supported by Office Document Imaging. As a result, if you want to turn a scanned document into Word text, you must save the scanned file in TIFF format. The imaging program can handle single- or multi-page TIFFs.

You can use any scanning program to create your TIFF file. Office 2003 comes with a program called Office Document Scanning, but you can use any other scanning program as long as it (and your scanning device) creates high-quality scans. The imaging program's ability to accurately decipher scanned text depends on both the resolution and the clarity of the scanned image. You'll also obtain better results if text in the original document is typewritten in a relatively simple and clear font. The imaging program is not designed to translate human handwriting or ornate typefaces.

Getting started

To start the imaging program, choose Start, Programs, Microsoft Office Tools, Microsoft Office Document Imaging.

The next step is to open the TIFF file you want to translate. Here's how:

1   Click the Open button on the toolbar (or choose File, Open) to open the Open dialog box.
2   Navigate to the folder that contains the TIFF file.
3   Select the relevant file.
4   Click Open.

At this point, the program window will appear as shown in Exhibit B-7. If you're working with a multi-page TIFF, the first page will appear in the right pane, and a series of thumbnail (or miniature) images will appear in the left pane. You can scroll among the various pages by clicking the thumbnails (or by using the Page arrows on the toolbar). If you're working with a single-page TIFF, there will be only one thumbnail image.

To change the magnification in the right pane, you have three options:

- Choose View, Zoom to open the Zoom dialog box, and then drag the slider to zoom in or out.
- Select the necessary magnification from the Zoom list.
- Click the Zoom In button or the Zoom Out button.

To view the document in full-screen mode, click the Reading View button on the toolbar, or choose View, Reading View. To get out of full-screen mode, press the Esc key.

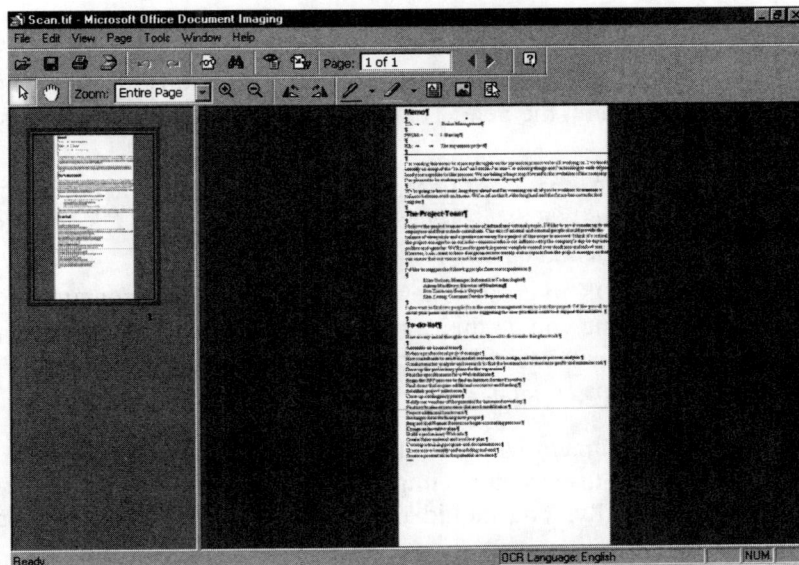

Exhibit B-7: The Office Document Imaging window with a sample scan

Sending an entire document to Word

If you want to send all of the scanned text to Word, here's what you do:

1 Click the Send Text to Word button (or choose Tools, Send Text to Word). After a moment, the Send Text to Word dialog box will appear, as shown in Exhibit B-8.

2 Select All pages, if necessary. (The first time you do this in the current TIFF file, the install OCR message box will appear. Click OK to proceed. You won't need the Office 2003 CD.)

3 Click OK to create a new Word document that contains the converted text. The first time you do this, a message box will indicate that the program must first decipher the text through a process called *optical character recognition* (OCR).

4 To proceed, click OK.

The Word document will not reflect the formatting of the original document, although paragraph and list structures might be maintained. In most cases, you'll need to format the text manually. You should also review the Word document carefully to ensure text accuracy.

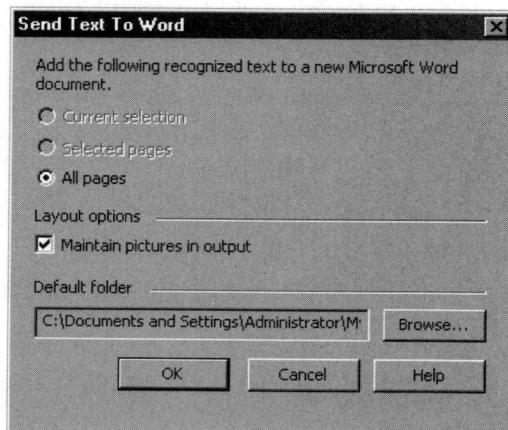

Exhibit B-8: The Send Text to Word dialog box

Sending part of a document to Word

If you don't need to re-create the entire document, you can send the scanned text to Word selectively. Here's how:

1 In the right pane, display the page that contains the text you want to send to Word.

2 Drag the mouse to draw a red box around the text.

3 Click the Send Text to Word button. After a moment, the Send Text to Word dialog box will appear. By default, Current selection is selected.

4 Click OK to create a new Word document containing the selected text. (The first time you do this in the current TIFF file, the OCR message box will appear. Click OK to proceed.)

Appendix C

Microsoft Office Specialist exam objectives maps

This appendix covers these additional topics:

A Word 2003 Specialist exam objectives with references to corresponding material in Course ILT courseware.

B Word 2003 Expert exam objectives with references to corresponding material in Course ILT courseware.

Topic A: Specialist exam objectives

The following table lists all Word 2003 Specialist exam objectives and provides a reference to the location of both the conceptual material and the activities that teach each objective.

Objective	Course level	Conceptual information	Supporting activities
Inserting text, symbols, hidden text and special characters	Basic	Unit 2, Topic C, pp 26-29	C-1, C-2
	Intermediate	Unit 7, Topic B, pp 18-19	B-3
Deleting, cutting, copying, pasting text and using the clipboard	Basic	Unit 3, Topic B, pp 8-12	B-1, B-2, B-3
Checking spelling and grammar	Basic	Unit 7, Topic A, pp 2-7	A-1, A-2, A-3
Checking language usage (e.g., Thesaurus)	Basic	Unit 7, Topic A, pp 8-10	A-4
Creating text for repeated use (e.g., AutoText)	Basic	Unit 2, Topic B, pp 21-22	B-5
Inserting pre-defined text (e.g., AutoText and AutoCorrect)	Basic	Unit 2, Topic B, pp 14-20	B-1, B-2, B-3, B-4
Inserting date and time fields	Basic	Unit 2, Topic C, pp 30-33	C-3
Finding and replacing text	Basic	Unit 3, Topic C, pp 13-17	C-1, C-2
Moving to selected content (e.g., Select Browse Object, Document Map)	Basic	Unit 2, Topic A, pp 8-10	A-4, A-5
	Intermediate	Unit 4, Topic C, pp 20-21	C-2
Inserting, positioning and sizing graphics, text boxes and shapes	Intermediate	Unit 7, Topic A, pp 2-8 Unit 7, Topic D, pp 26-30, 32-33	A-1, A-2, A-3 D-1, D-3
Creating and modifying charts and diagrams	Intermediate	Unit 3, Topic A, pp 6-9 Unit 7, Topic D, pp 34-37	A-3, A-4 D-4
Locating supporting information in local reference materials or on the Internet using the Research tool	Basic	Unit 1, Topic C, pp 16-21	C-1, C-2, C-3
Using the Research tool to select and insert supporting text-based information	Basic	Unit 7, Topic A, pp 8-10	A-4
Inserting new tables	Basic	Unit 5, Topic A, pp 2-4	A-1, A-2
Converting text to tables	Basic	Unit 5, Topic A, pp 5-6	A-3
Applying pre-defined formats to tables (e.g., AutoFormats)	Intermediate	Unit 2, Topic C, pp 16-17	C-1
Modifying table borders and shading	Intermediate	Unit 2, Topic B, pp 13-15	B-1, B-2

Objective	Course level	Conceptual information	Supporting activities
Revising tables (insert and delete rows and columns, modify cell formats)	Basic	Unit 5, Topic C, pp 12-17	C-1, C-2, C-3
Customizing and applying bullets and numbering	Basic	Unit 4, Topic C, pp 32-35	C-3, C-4
Creating outlines	Intermediate	Unit 4, Topic C, pp 18-19	C-1
Inserting and modifying hyperlinks to other documents and Web pages	Basic	Unit 8, Topic B, pp 10-13	B-1, B-2, B-3
Finding and modifying font typeface, style, color and size	Basic	Unit 4, Topic A, pp 2-6	A-1, A-2
Applying styles to and clearing styles from text, tables, and lists	Intermediate	Unit 4, Topic A, pp 2-11 Unit 4, Topic B, p 16	A-1, A-2, A-3, A-4, A-5 B-3
Applying highlights to text	Basic	Unit 4, Topic A, p 9	A-4
Applying text effects	Basic	Unit 4, Topic A, pp 7-8	A-3
Modifying character spacing	Basic	Unit 4, Topic A, pp 7-8	A-3
Applying borders and shading to paragraphs	Basic	Unit 4, Topic C, pp 30-31	C-2
Indenting, spacing and aligning paragraphs	Basic	Unit 4, Topic C, pp 27-29 Unit 4, Topic D, pp 37-40, 42-45	C-1 D-1, D-2, D-4, D-5
Setting, removing and modifying tab stops	Basic	Unit 4, Topic B, pp 20-26	B-1, B-2, B-3, B-4
Applying and formatting columns	Intermediate	Unit 1, Topic B, pp 7-12, 14 Unit 1, Topic C, pp 15-16	B-1, B-2, B-3, B-5 C-1
Inserting and modifying content in document headers and footers	Basic	Unit 6, Topic A, pp 2-6	A-1, A-2, A-3
	Intermediate	Unit 5, Topic A, pp 2-8	A-1, A-2, A-3
Inserting and formatting page numbers	Intermediate	Unit 5, Topic B, pp 9-16	B-1, B-2, B-3, B-4
Inserting and deleting breaks	Basic	Unit 6, Topic C, pp 16-18	C-1, C-2
	Intermediate	Unit 1, Topic A, p 2-4 Unit 1, Topic B, pp 10-11, 13	A-1 B-2, B-4
Modifying page margins, page orientation	Basic	Unit 6, Topic B, pp 7-13	B-1, B-2, B-3
Sending documents for review via e-mail	Basic	Unit 8, Topic C, pp 14-15	C-1

Objective	Course level	Conceptual information	Supporting activities
Sending documents in an e-mail or as an e-mail attachment	Basic	Unit 8, Topic C, pp 14-15	C-1
Comparing and merging documents	Intermediate	Unit 9, Topic A, pp 12-13 Unit 9, Topic C, p 23	A-5 C-3
Inserting, viewing and editing comments	Intermediate	Unit 9, Topic B, pp 14-17, 19	B-1, B-2, B-3, B-5
Locating successive changes in a document	Intermediate	Unit 9, Topic A, pp 6-7	A-2
Tracking, accepting and rejecting changes	Intermediate	Unit 9, Topic A, pp 2-7	A-1, A-2
Creating new document types using templates	Intermediate	Unit 8, Topic A, pp 2-4	A-1
Reviewing and modifying the document summary	Intermediate	Unit 8, Topic B, pp 14-15	B-3
Reviewing word, paragraph and character counts (e.g., Word Count)	Intermediate	Unit 8, Topic B, pp 14-15	B-3
Creating and using folders for document storage	Basic	Unit 1, Topic B, p 12	B-4
Renaming folders	Basic	Unit 1, Topic B, p 15	B-7
Converting documents to different formats for transportability (e.g., .rtf, .txt)	Basic	Unit 1, Topic B, p 12	None
Saving documents as Web pages	Basic	Unit 8, Topic A, pp 4-5	A-2
Printing documents, envelopes, and labels	Intermediate Basic	Unit 6, Topic A, pp 2-5 Unit 7, Topic B, pp 14-15	A-1, A-2 B-2
Previewing a document for printing	Basic	Unit 7, Topic B, pp 11-13	B-1
Previewing a Web page for publication	Basic	Unit 8, Topic A, pp 2-3	A-1
Revealing formatting and hidden text	Basic	Unit 1, Topic B, pp 8-9 Unit 4, Topic A, pp 15-17	B-2 A-8

Objective	Course level	Conceptual information	Supporting activities
Viewing reading layout, normal, outline, full screen, zoom views	Basic	Unit 2, Topic A, pp 12-13 Unit 7, Topic B, pp 11-12	A-7 B-1
	Intermediate	Unit 4, Topic C, pp 18-19	C-1
Showing/hiding white space in a document	Basic	Unit 2, Topic A, p 11	A-6
Splitting windows and arrange panes	Intermediate	Unit 7, Topic B, pp 16-17	B-2

Topic B: Expert exam objectives

Explanation

The following table lists all Word 2003 Expert exam objectives and provides a reference to the location of both the conceptual material and the activities that teach each objective.

Objective	Course level	Conceptual information	Supporting activities
Creating and applying custom styles for text, tables and lists	Intermediate	Unit 4, Topic A, pp 2-11	A-1, A-2, A-3, A-4, A-5
Controlling orphans and widows	Basic	Unit 6, Topic B, pp 14-15	B-4
Setting line and page breaks	Basic	Unit 4, Topic D, p 41 Unit 6, Topic C, pp 16-18	D-3 C-1, C-2
Wrapping text with graphics	Intermediate	Unit 7, Topic A, pp 12-13	A-6
Cropping and rotating graphics	Intermediate	Unit 7, Topic A, pp 6-7 Unit 7, Topic D, pp 26-30	None D-1
Controlling image contrast and brightness	Intermediate	Unit 7, Topic A, p 9	A-4
Scaling and resizing graphics	Intermediate	Unit 7, Topic A, pp 6-8	A-3
Inserting and modifying new objects and objects from files	Intermediate	Unit 7, Topic A, pp 2-11 Unit 7, Topic B, pp 14-15	A-1, A-2, A-3, A-4, A-5 B-1
Creating and revising charts using data from other sources (e.g., Excel)	Intermediate	Unit 3, Topic A, pp 2-9	A-1, A-2, A-3, A-4
Sorting content in lists and tables by specific categories	Intermediate	Unit 1, Topic C, pp 17-18	C-2
Using formulas in tables	Intermediate	Unit 3, Topic B, pp 10-15	B-1, B-2, B-3
Modifying table formats by merging and/or splitting table cells	Intermediate	Unit 2, Topic A, pp 5-7	A-2
Modifying text position and direction in a cell	Intermediate	Unit 2, Topic A, pp 8-9	A-3
Modifying table properties	Basic	Unit 5, Topic C, pp 16-18	C-3, C-4
	Intermediate	Unit 2, Topic A, p 10	A-4
Inserting and modifying fields	Intermediate	Unit 8, Topic B, pp 18-21	B-5, B-6
Summarizing relevant content using automated tools (e.g., AutoSummarize)	Advanced	Unit 3, Topic A, pp 14-16	A-7

Objective	Course level	Conceptual information	Supporting activities
Analyzing content readability using automated tools (e.g., Readability Statistics)	Advanced	Unit 3, Topic A, pp 14-16	A-7
Inserting bookmarks	Advanced	Unit 3, Topic D, pp 27-28	D-1
Using automation features for document navigation (e.g., Document Map, Thumbnails)	Intermediate	Unit 4, Topic C, pp 20-22	C-2, C-3
Completing an entire mail merge process for form letters	Advanced	Unit 1, Topic A, pp 2-11 Unit 1, Topic B, pp 12-16	A-1, A-2, A-3 B-1
Completing an entire mail merge process for mailing labels	Advanced	Unit 1, Topic C, p 21-24	C-1, C-2
Adding, deleting, updating and modifying schemas, solutions and settings in the Schema Library	Advanced	Unit 6, Topic A, pp 5-12	A-2, A-3
Adding, deleting, and modifying schemas and transforms to documents	Advanced	Unit 6, Topic A, pp 5-10, 13-17	A-2, A-4, A-5
Managing elements and attributes in XML documents (e.g., adding, changing deleting, cutting, copying)	Advanced	Unit 6, Topic A, pp 5-10	A-2
Defining XML options (e.g., applying schema validation options, applying XML view options)	Advanced	Unit 6, Topic A, pp 11-12	A-3
Creating and modifying forms	Advanced	Unit 2, Topic A, pp 5-8 Unit 2, Topic B, pp 18-21	A-2, A-3 B-1, B-2, B-3
Setting and changing options on form fields and check boxes	Advanced	Unit 2, Topic A, pp 9-17	A-4, A-5, A-6, A-7
Creating watermarks	Intermediate	Unit 7, Topic C, p 24	C-2
Applying themes	Intermediate	Unit 7, Topic C, p 25	C-3
Creating and modifying document background colors and fill effects	Intermediate	Unit 7, Topic C, pp 20-23	C-1
Creating and modifying document indexes, tables of content, figures, and authorities	Advanced	Unit 3, Topic A, pp 7-8, 12-13 Unit 3, Topic C, pp 23-26	A-4, A-6 C-1, C-2
Inserting format and modifying endnotes, footnotes, captions, and cross-references	Advanced	Unit 3, Topic A, pp 9-11 Unit 3, Topic B, pp 17-22 Unit 3, Topic D, pp 30-31	A-5 B-1, B-2, B-3, B-4 D-4
Formatting numbering and marks for footnotes and endnotes	Advanced	Unit 3, Topic B, pp 17-18, 20-21	B-1, B-3

Objective	Course level	Conceptual information	Supporting activities
Creating master documents with three or more subdocuments	Advanced	Unit 3, Topic A, pp 2-3	A-1
Setting reviewer's ink colors, setting balloon options, showing and hiding reviewers	Intermediate	Unit 9, Topic A, pp 2-5, 8-9	A-1, A-3
Setting Web options and saving to a Web server	Basic	Unit 8, Topic A, p 4	None
Inserting and modifying frames	Advanced	Unit 3, Topic E, pp 32-37	E-1, E-2
Creating, viewing, deleting versions of documents	Intermediate	Unit 9, Topic C, pp 20-23	C-1, C-2, C-3
Setting formatting restrictions	Intermediate	Unit 8, Topic B, pp 22-26	B-7
Setting editing restrictions	Intermediate	Unit 9, Topic A, pp 10-11	A-4
Adding users excepted from restrictions (groups and individuals)	Advanced	Unit 2, Topic C, pp 26-28	C-3
Applying passwords to documents and forms	Intermediate	Unit 8, Topic B, pp 10-13	B-2
	Advanced	Unit 2, Topic C, pp 22-24	C-1
Using digital signatures to authenticate documents	Advanced	Unit 2, Topic D, pp 32-33	D-1
Inserting and editing summary and custom information in document properties	Intermediate	Unit 8, Topic B, pp 14-15	B-3
Creating and running macros	Advanced	Unit 4, Topic A, pp 2-5, 7 Unit 4, Topic C, pp 13-15	A-1, A-3 C-1
Editing a macro using the Visual Basic Editor	Advanced	Unit 4, Topic B, p 8	B-1
Creating a custom menu	Advanced	Unit 5, Topic A, pp 2-7	A-1, A-2
Adding and removing buttons from a toolbar	Advanced	Unit 5, Topic B, pp 10-15	B-1, B-2, B-3
Changing the default file location for templates	Intermediate	Unit 8, Topic B, pp 8-9	B-1
Setting default dictionary	Basic	Unit 7, Topic A, p 4	None
Modifying default font settings	Basic	Unit 4, Topic A, pp 5-6	A-2

Course summary

This summary contains information to help you bring the course to a successful conclusion. Using this information, you will be able to:

A Use the summary text to reinforce what you've learned in class.

B Determine the next courses in this series (if any), as well as any other resources that might help you continue to learn about Microsoft Word 2003.

Topic A: Course summary

Use the following summary text to reinforce what you've learned in class.

Unit summaries

Unit 1

You learned about the various parts of the **Word environment**. Then you learned how to **enter text** in a blank document and how to **save** a document. Next, you learned how to **close** a document and **create a new document**. Finally, you learned how to use the **Help** system.

Unit 2

You learned how to **open** a document and **scroll** and **move** in a long document. Next, you learned how to use **AutoCorrect** and the **AutoCorrect Options button**. Then, you learned how to **insert an AutoText entry** and **create an AutoText entry**. Next, you learned how to **move the insertion point** and **insert** and **delete text**. You also learned how to insert the date and time by using the **Date and Time dialog box** and the **date smart tag**. Finally, you learned how to use **Undo** and **Redo**.

Unit 3

You learned how to **select text** in a document by using the keyboard and the mouse. Then you learned how to **copy** and **move text** within a document and between documents. Finally, you learned how to **find** and **replace text**.

Unit 4

You learned how to **apply bold, italic**, and **underline** formats to text. You also learned how to **change** the **font** and **font size**. You learned how to apply **superscript, subscript**, and **text animation effects**. Next, you learned how to **use tabs** in a document. Then you learned how to **align paragraphs** and **apply bullets** and **numbering** to lists. Finally, you learned how to work with **indents, line spacing**, and **paragraph spacing**.

Unit 5

You learned how to **create tables, select table elements**, and **enter text in a table**. Then you learned how to **add** and **delete columns** and **rows, delete a table**, and **change column widths**. Finally, you learned how to **format text in a table** and **align a table** on the page.

Unit 6

You learned how to **add text** and **AutoText** to **headers** and **footers**. Then you learned how to **set** and **change margins** by using Print Preview and the Page Setup dialog box. Finally, you learned how to **add** and **delete page breaks**.

Unit 7

You learned how to **proof documents** by using the **Spelling** and **Grammar** features. You also learned how to use the **Thesaurus** to find alternative words.

Unit 8

You learned how to save a Word document as a **Web Page (HTML)** and a **Single File Web Page (MHTML)**. You also learned how to **view the HTML file in a browser**. You learned how to **insert hyperlinks** to other documents. You also learned how to **e-mail Word documents** to other people.

Topic B: Continued learning after class

It is impossible to learn to use any software effectively in a single day. To get the most out of this class, you should begin working with Word 2003 to perform real tasks as soon as possible. Course Technology also offers resources for continued learning.

Next courses in this series

This is the first course in this series. The next courses in this series are:

- *Word 2003: Intermediate*
- *Word 2003: Advanced*

Other resources

You might find some of these other resources useful as you continue to learn about Word 2003. For more information, visit www.course.com.

- *Microsoft Word 2003 Fast & Easy*
  ISBN: 1592000800

Word 2003:
Basic
Quick reference

Button	Shortcut keys	Function
	CTRL + N	Opens a new blank document.
	CTRL + O	Displays the Open dialog box, used to open existing documents.
	CTRL + S	Saves changes in a document. If used for the first time, opens the Save As dialog box.
	CTRL + P	Prints a document.
	CTRL + F2	Used to preview a document before printing it.
	F7	Opens the Spelling and Grammar dialog box, used to check the spelling in a document.
	CTRL + s + O	Opens the Research task pane.
	CTRL + X	Cuts text from a document.
	CTRL + C	Copies text from a document.
	CTRL + V	Pastes text into a document.
	CTRL + SHIFT + C	Copies the format of the selected text.
	CTRL + Z	Undoes previous actions.
	CTRL + Y	Redoes previous actions.

Button	Shortcut keys	Function
	CTRL + K	Opens the Insert Hyperlink dialog box.
		Inserts a table.
¶	CTRL + SHIFT + F8	Displays or hides nonprinting characters.
	F1	Displays the Microsoft Word Help task pane.
B	CTRL + B	Applies a bold format to text.
I	CTRL + I	Applies italics to text.
U	CTRL + U	Applies an underline to text.
	CTRL + L	Aligns text to the left.
	CTRL + E	Centers text.
	CTRL + R	Aligns text to the right.
	CTRL + J	Justifies text.
		Adjusts line spacing
		Applies numbering to the selected paragraphs.
		Applies bullets to the selected paragraphs.
		Inserts the page number in the header or footer area.
		Inserts the document's total number of pages in the header or footer area.
		Inserts the current system date.
		Inserts the current system time.

Button	Shortcut keys	Function
		Opens the Page Setup dialog box.
		Switches between the header and footer of a page.
		Creates a new folder.
		Displays or hides multiple pages in Reading Layout view.
		Displays the various AutoCorrect options.

Glossary

Antonym

A word with the opposite meaning.

AutoCorrect

A feature that corrects common errors as you type, such as misspelled words and incorrect capitalization.

AutoFormat

A feature that applies formatting—such as headings, bulleted and numbered lists, borders, symbols, and fractions—based on the AutoFormat settings in the AutoCorrect dialog box.

Automatic page break

Inserted by Word when the amount of text exceeds the vertical margins. Automatic page breaks appear as widely spaced dotted lines

AutoText

A feature that inserts predefined text entries, such as salutations, headers, footers, and signatures.

Cell

The intersection of a row and a column.

Character formats

Used to improve the appearance of documents, character formats include fonts, font styles, and font sizes.

Click and Type

A feature that uses the mouse pointer to insert text, graphics, and other items in a document with automatically applied paragraph formatting.

Document area

The large area that contains the insertion point where you type and edit text.

End-of-document marker

A small, black horizontal line that appears below the insertion point. .

Font

The design of the characters. (Can also be called *typeface*). Two commonly used fonts are Times New Roman and Arial.

Font styles

Include bold, italic, and underline that is applied to fonts. (Can also be called *type styles.*)

Footer

Text that prints at the bottom of the page.

Format Painter

A button, on the Standard toolbar, that copies the formatting of text and applies it to other text you select.

Formatting toolbar

Contains buttons you can use for formatting text, such as changing font and font size.

Gridlines

Provide a visual reference for the table's rows and columns. The gridlines are not visible when you print a document.

Hanging indents

Affect all the lines in a paragraph except the first line. You use hanging indents for lists and to set off a paragraph. All the lines below the first line are indented.

Header

Text that prints at the top of the page.

Hyperlinks

Words or graphics that are used to navigate the Web. A hyperlink can lead you to another location on the same Web page or to another Web page.

Hypertext Markup Language (HTML)

Special code that is used in a document to control how it will appear in a Web browser.

Indent

Define the left and right sides of a paragraph relative to the margins of the page. By default, indents are set to match the left and right margins.

Insertion point

A flashing vertical line in the document area.

Leader

A series of characters (such as dots or dashes) that fill in the spaces between tabbed text. Dot leaders are commonly used in tables of contents.

Line spacing

Controls the amount of vertical space between the lines of a paragraph.

Manual page breaks

Inserted by you to start a new page. Manual page breaks appear as closely spaced dotted lines with the words "Page Break" inserted in the middle of the line.

Margins

Define the amount of space between the text and the upper, lower, left, and right edges of the page. By default, the top and bottom margins are set at 1" and the left and right margins at 1.25".

Menu bar

Displays all menus available in Word. Each menu consists of a set of logically grouped commands.

Nonprinting characters

Symbols that appear on the screen to represent actions on the keyboard, such as the Enter key, the Tab key, and spacebar.

Object

Document elements such as pages, sections, comments, tables, or graphics.

Office Assistant

An animated help system that can answer questions while you work.

Office Clipboard

A temporary storage area that collects cut or copied text until you specify where to place it. The Office Clipboard appears in the Clipboard task pane, and can hold up to 24 items.

Orphan

A paragraph's first line printed by itself at the bottom of a page.

Overtype mode

Used to replace existing text, character by character, with the text you type.

Page break

A separator that is inserted to create a new page when there is more text on a page than the margins can accommodate.

Page orientation

Controls whether the text on the page is set to print as 8.5" x 11" (portrait) or 11" x 8.5" (landscape). Most business documents have a portrait orientation.

Pagination

The process of separating text into pages.

Paragraph spacing

Controls the amount of vertical space between paragraphs.

Print Preview

Feature that helps you see on the screen what your document will look like when it's printed.

Ruler

The horizontal and vertical rulers are used to set and view paragraph indents, tab stops, page margins, and column widths.

Sans serif font

Lacks the small lines of a serif font, and works well for headings because the lack of lines at the top and base of the letters makes the text stand out.

Save AutoRecover

An automatic save feature that can be set to ensure that documents are saved regularly. The settings are found on the Save tab in the Options dialog box.

Selecting text

Highlighting it by using the mouse, the keyboard, or a menu command.

Selection bar

Located on the left side of the document window, it's useful for selecting lines, paragraphs, or an entire document. When the mouse pointer changes to a right-pointing arrow, click the mouse button to select a line; double-click to select a paragraph; or click and drag to select multiple lines.

Serif font

Has small lines at the top and bottom of letters.

Scrollbars

Shaded bars displayed along the right side and the bottom of the document window. Used to move in a document, such as a multi-page report that cannot fit completely in the document area.

Smart tags

Indicated by the purple dotted lines that appear beneath text, smart tags identify specific types of information, such as dates, and provide you with a list of related actions, such as scheduling a meeting.

Standard toolbar

Contains buttons for frequently used actions, such as opening files, saving files, and copying and pasting text. The buttons on this toolbar are shortcuts to the commands available in the menus.

Status bar

Located at the bottom of the screen, it displays information about the current document, such as the total number of pages, the number of the current page, and the position of the insertion point.

Style

A collection of various formats that can be applied, in one step, to paragraphs, characters, or tables.

Synonym

A word with the same or similar meaning.

Table

An excellent way to present information in a column layout by using rows and columns.

Tab stops

Predefined locations on the ruler. Each time you press the Tab key, the text is automatically moved to the first tab stop on the ruler.

Task pane

A dynamic area on the right side of the screen that provides shortcuts for performing commonly used commands, such as creating documents or formatting text. Word provides 14 task panes.

Thesaurus

A tool that provides alternatives, or synonyms, for words.

Title bar

Displays the program title and the name of the current document.

View buttons

Found to the left of the horizontal scrollbar, they are used to change the view of the current document. The View buttons are Normal, Web Layout, Print Layout, Outline, and Reading Layout. These commands can also be found in the View menu.

Web browser

Software used to access Web sites, which contain Web pages.

Widow

A paragraph's last line printed by itself at the beginning of a page.

Word processor

A program that helps you create, edit, format, and print documents such as letters, reports, and Web pages.

Word-wrap

When typing, as you reach the end of a line of text, the insertion point (and text) automatically moves to the next line of the document.

Index